INTRODUCTION	3
II	**ORIGINATION OF THE RESPONSES**	7
	LEA BY LEA	7
	AS A PERCENTAGE OF THE TOTAL	8
III	**SUMMARY OF THE FINDINGS**	11
	1 THE SCHOOLS	11
	2 THE TEACHERS	13
	3 FINANCE AND RESOURCES	14
	4 THE ORGANISATION OF CAREERS EDUCATION	16
	5 TIME	17
	6 EXTERNAL FACTORS	19
IV	**THE ANALYSIS**	23
V	**GENERAL IMPRESSIONS**	87
VI	**CONCLUSIONS**	93
VII	**RECOMMENDATIONS**	97
VIII	**APPENDICES**	99
	1 BIBLIOGRAPHY	99
	2 THE ORIGINAL QUESTIONNAIRE	100
	3 NACGT	110
	4 THE NEWPOINT PUBLISHING COMPANY LIMITED	112

This page has been intentionally left blank

I INTRODUCTION

In 1973 'Survey 18 - Careers Education in Secondary Schools' was published. The information from the Survey, undertaken by Her Majesty's Inspectors (HMI), painted a fairly damning picture of the state of careers in British schools in the early 1970s. At that time, in their response to the publication, the National Association of Careers and Guidance Teachers (NACGT) stated: 'It is deplorable that after all has been written about the need for adequate careers guidance the HMIs should have found that 'The concept of careers education is not at present, generally accepted or put into practice except by a minority of schools'!'

Since the publication of Survey 18 by the Department of Education and Science, much more - one could almost say whole libraries - has been written extolling the virtue of school provision of good careers education and guidance.

But the question which has remained on the lips of many practitioners, particularly those who have been around for some time, is 'Has the situation improved since 1973?' It was anticipated that the Department of Education and Science (DES) would follow up Survey 18 with a similar survey in the late 1970s or early 1980s. However, this has never transpired despite the seemingly endless pronouncements by the government, and by government and quasi-government agencies, about the importance of careers education and guidance. No one, or so it appeared, was prepared to take stock of the situation.

Neither was any significant attempt made to check, no matter how subjectively, whether the recommendations made in Survey 18 had been implemented. Whilst it is important to recognise that changes have taken place in educational thinking over the past 15 years or so, and some variation in the meaning of careers education is therefore to be expected, what remains consistent is the need for the training of teachers to enable them to undertake activities inexorably linked with the careers education and guidance process.

One of the more significant sections of Survey 18 is that concerned with the in-service training of 'careers teachers' (In-service training 177):

> 'There is a pressing need for an expanded and well co-ordinated programme of in-service training. Two recommendations are offered:
> - In the longer term it is reasonable to expect that the provision of one-year diploma courses at present designed primarily for counsellors will be expanded, and that some of them will accommodate teachers wishing to be concerned with educational and vocational guidance as well as those whose aptitude and temperament incline them towards personal and social aspects of the work.

- In the short term, every designated careers
  teacher, before taking up duties as such, should
  attend a preparatory course of at least one
  week's duration. This should be followed up,
  within the next two years, by further in-service
  training preferably over an extended period. All
  teachers already in posts but not having attended
  any such course should be given the facility to
  do so at the earliest opportunity.'

So how far have these two recommendations been taken on board
by central government, local education authorities and schools
in the decade or so since the publication of the DES Report of
the Survey undertaken by HMI?

One other feature of Survey 18 was the inclusion of
'Guidelines' and it is only proper to question the extent to
which attempts have been made to monitor and publish schools
careers work as outlined in these Guidelines.

'A school providing good careers education may be
expected to display the following features:
- a policy of careers education for all pupils;
- a curriculum that keeps doors open;
- a pastoral system of which careers education
  forms an integral part;

- careers work co-ordinated by a nominated teacher
  with the necessary training, experience and
  status;
- active involvement of other members of staff in
  careers work, and effective communication between
  all concerned with the curriculum and with
  pastoral care;
- time made available both for teachers and pupils;
- an effective working relationship with the
  careers office, with higher and further
  education, and with the world of employment;
- adequate collection and storage of information
  about all pupils;
- effective discussion between the pupil and all
  concerned with guidance - parents, teachers and
  careers officers;
- adequate accommodation and resources, well used'
                                        (Paragraph 194)

Expectations of a follow-up study to the investigation were
high, and disappointment prevailed when none emerged. How were
we to know how adequate the current state of careers was,
particularly when its importance was continually being
stressed to us, and it was appearing as a compulsory element
in many curriculum innovations?

It was, then, against this background that I volunteered to
'survey the current situation' on behalf of the NACGT, which

resulted in many schools receiving the questionnaire at the time of the initial closing date (21 May). Fortunately the media published information extending the deadline, and completed questionnaires continued to be returned throughout the summer.

The response to the Survey has been overwhelming. The earliest predictions estimated a return of 250-300 replies which would be statistically valid. However, over 900 replies were received providing a plethora of data which was processed by YTS trainees at Hastings Information Technology Centre allowing for ease of analysis.

What follows are the results of that analysis, which it is hoped will help everyone concerned with the preparation of young people for adulthood to understand the state of careers in the UK in 1986. However, it must be emphasised that the data included in this report is based on what careers teachers have stated and no attempt has been made to check the accuracy of the statements. All that can be presented is a quantitative analysis and not a qualitative one. However, in no way should it be inferred that the information contained in this Report is inaccurate. The consistency of the responses clearly does not support such a view.

David Cleaton

This page has been intentionally left blank

LEA BY LEA

ENGLISH SHIRE COUNTIES

Avon	15
Bedfordshire	6
Berkshire	5
Buckinghamshire	13
Cambridgeshire	8
Cheshire	14
Cleveland	8
Cornwall	6
Cumbria	10
Derbyshire	20
Devon	17
Dorset	5
Durham	5
East Sussex	23
Essex	21
Gloucestershire	17
Hampshire	24
Hereford & Worcester	9
Hertfordshire	18
Humberside	11
Isle of Man	1
Isle of Wight	3
Kent	22
Lancashire	29
Leicestershire	12
Lincolnshire	14
Norfolk	15
North Yorkshire	10
Northamptonshire	7
Northumberland	2
Nottinghamshire	16
Oxfordshire	9
Shropshire	6
Somerset	11
Staffordshire	16
Suffolk	8
Surrey	11
Warwickshire	10
West Sussex	6
Wiltshire	8

	471

Independent schools	76
Other	7

METROPOLITAN BOROUGHS

Barnsley	4
Birmingham	16
Bolton	4
Bradford	8
Bury	5
Calderdale	3
Coventry	2
Doncaster	1
Dudley	4
Gateshead	1
Kirklees	6
Knowsley	3
Leeds	5
Liverpool	8
Manchester	6
Newcastle	0
North Tyneside	3
Oldham	3
Rochdale	2
Rotherham	1
St Helens	4
Salford	3
Sandwell	6
Sefton	15
Sheffield	10
Solihull	2
South Tyneside	2
Stockport	1
Sunderland	10

Tameside	3	Mid Glamorgan	22
Trafford	4	Powys	6
Wakefield	2	South Glamorgan	13
Walsall	1	West Glamorgan	4
Wigan	6		-------
Wirral	5		60
Wolverhampton	7		-------

	166		

SCOTLAND

Borders	2
Dumfries & Galloway	4
Fife	2
Grampian	5
Highland	0
Lothian	6
Orkney	1
Shetland	0
Strathclyde	9
Tayside	5
Western Isles	0

	34

LONDON

ILEA	30
Barking	0
Barnet	3
Bexley	2
Brent	6
Bromley	6
Croydon	4
Ealing	2
Enfield	4
Haringey	4
Harrow	3
Havering	7
Hillingdon	4
Hounslow	5
Kingston	3
Merton	3
Newham	3
Redbridge	4
Richmond	3
Sutton	4
Waltham Forest	2

	102

AS A PERCENTAGE OF THE TOTAL

Shire counties	471	51%
Metropolitan boroughs	166	18%
London (ILEA & boroughs)	102	11%
Wales	60	7%
Scotland	34	4%
Independents	76	8%
Other	7	1%
	--------	--------
	916	100%
	--------	--------

WALES

Clwyd	3
Dyfed	2
Gwent	8
Gwynedd	2

TVEI RETURNS

Shire counties	48%
Metropolitan boroughs	33%
London (ILEA & boroughs)	15%
Wales	16%
Scotland	8%

14% of all shire county returns
20% of all metropolitan borough returns
15% of all London returns
27% of all Welsh returns
 8% of all Scottish returns

This page has been intentionally left blank

III SUMMARY OF THE FINDINGS

The information gleaned from the completed questionnaires has been analysed and divided into nine comparable groupings, ie

- the total survey
- all local education authorities
- independent schools
- schools in English shire counties
- schools in metropolitan boroughs
- schools in the Inner London Education Authority (ILEA) and the London boroughs (described as London in this Report)
- schools in Scotland
- schools in Wales
- Technical and Vocational Education Initiative (TVEI) schools (in England, Wales and Scotland)

A small number (1% of the total) of questionnaires was received which, although fitting into the total Survey, did not fit into any of the sub groups. These included questionnaires from the Isle of Man, the Channel Isles and Youth Custody Centres. One or two questionnaires did not indicate the designation of the school or the LEA and are, therefore, included in the 'other' category.

For the purposes of this Report all institutions which returned a questionnaire, whatever their designation, are referred to as schools.

Not all respondents answered every question, but to make it easier to read and compare the results, the data, with just a few exceptions, appears as a percentage.

The responses to two questions (6.4 (a) and 6.5 (a)) are not included in this Report. It did not prove possible, due to the inadequacy of the questions, to provide the data in a sensible and coherent format.

It should also be added that although the format of this Report makes comparison between the groupings relatively easy eg between London and Scotland, this is not the purpose of the Report. What should prove possible is for a teacher in one location (eg a metropolitan borough) to compare the institution in which they work with other institutions of the same grouping.

What follows is a description of the findings of the Survey. The figures in brackets refer to the number of the question on the questionnaire which is reproduced in full as an appendix to the Report. All the statistical data to which reference is made appears in Section IV of this Report.

1 THE SCHOOLS

1.1 Participants in the Survey were asked to provide information about the size (1.1), age range (1.2), designation (1.3) and catchment area (1.4) of the schools.

This information showed a good range of schools involved in the Survey and appears to be fairly representative of both the country as a whole as well as any particular grouping.

With the exception of the independent schools there is a very good correlation between the various groupings as far as size of schools is concerned. Again with the exception of the independent schools and this time Scotland, there is a clear correlation as far as the designation of the schools is concerned. (Time and time again in this Report the sharp difference between the Scottish education system and that of England and Wales will be exposed.) All the schools in the Survey from Scotland and Wales were comprehensive, but the correlation between the different types of schools in the other groupings was, again, very high.

As would be expected there are wide differences in the catchment areas of the various groupings.

1.2 The next questions which the schools were asked concerned involvement in TVEI (1.5) and CPVE (1.6).

As far as TVEI involvement is concerned, the figure for shire counties is low, at 15%, compared with most of the other groupings which are all over 20%. The larger numbers involved in the Survey from the shire counties brings the percentage for the whole Survey down to 16%. It must be remembered that independent schools are not involved in TVEI.

There is a degree of consistency about participation in CPVE although in Scotland (at 15%) it is very low and in Wales (68%) very high. TVEI schools (58%) also show considerable involvement in CPVE.

1.3 The next group of questions was about school policy (1.7) and LEA policy (1.9 and 1.10) regarding careers education.

There is a reasonable correlation between the groupings as far as the existence of a written policy for a school's careers education is concerned.

71% of schools have a written policy statement for careers education.

However, it is quite remarkable that 3% of the respondents (11% in London) did not know if their school had a written policy statement for careers education.

Consistently over one third of careers teachers do not know if their LEA has a written policy for careers education.

A great deal of confusion appears to prevail amongst teachers about LEA policy towards careers education. Teachers in the same authority consistently contradicted each other both as to whether the LEA had a written policy for careers education and as to whether the LEA had an inspector/adviser for careers education.

59% of LEAs are said to have an adviser/inspector for careers education, but

12% of careers teachers do not know if their LEA has an adviser/inspector for careers education.

Even more confusion prevails with the answers to the question about whether the adviser/inspector shares this responsibility with responsibility for another subject. Significant contradictions are made within LEAs.

However, from the data provided, it can be seen that

51% of LEAs have an adviser/inspector for careers education who shares this role with responsibility for another subject or subjects.

2 THE TEACHERS

The next section of questions was concerned with the number of teachers formally involved in careers work in each institution (2.1); the designation of the teachers (2.2); if they are members of NACGT (2.3); salary levels; status within the school (2.6 & 2.7); equivalent number of careers teachers (2.8); and the training received (2.9).

2.1 There appears to be very little difference between any of the groupings as far as the number of teachers involved in careers work in any one school is concerned. The norm seems to be either up to four teachers or more than 10. There is a slight variation in Scotland, but, almost certainly, this is accounted for by the system of 'guidance teachers' which exists 'north of the border'.

2.2 **70% of those teachers involved in careers work are designated as careers teachers** although this is much lower in independent schools (16%) and Scotland (28%).

2.3 **24% of the respondents to the survey were members of the NACGT.**

The only marked variation in NACGT membership within the groups was Scotland with 2%. (This reflects very accurately NACGT membership in Scotland compared with that in England and Wales.)

2.4 **53% of teachers involved in careers work are paid an allowance for this work.**

The only significant variations in this are independent schools (38%) and Wales (24%).

2.5 Excluding Scotland (which has a different pay structure), there is a very high correlation of salary scales paid to careers teachers in state schools. Some variations exist between state schools and independent schools at the lower end of the pay scales.

58% of the senior careers teachers in schools are on Scale 3 salaries or less.

29% are on Scale 4 salaries.

However, only 36% of teachers receive an extra allowance exclusively for careers work.

2.6 **In 83% of schools the senior careers teacher is regarded as a head of department.**

2.7 However despite the high percentage who are regarded as head of department only

16% are always involved in school management decisions, although a further 36% usually participate, and

37% always sit on the school's curriculum committee although a further 26% are usually involved.

2.8 **60% of schools have the equivalent of less than one full-time careers teacher.**

A further 35% of schools have the equivalent of between one and two full-time careers teachers.

There is little variation in these statistics although TVEI schools are marginally better staffed on the careers side.

2.9 The statistics for training show a remarkably high degree of correlation across all groupings and present one of the most depressing pictures uncovered by this Survey.

41% of careers teachers have received less than five days of training for careers work.

68% of careers teachers have received less than 20 days of training for careers work.

Only 4% of careers teachers have received a full-time one-year course of training for careers work.

3 FINANCE AND RESOURCES

Questions in Section 3 of the Survey questionnaire were concerned with the allocation of finance to the careers department (3.1); physical resources (3.2); equipment available and the extent to which it is used (3.3); the availability of information technology systems (3.4); the existence of a careers information area (3.5) and the use of careers information (3.6).

3.1 The allocation of finance to the careers departments seems to be either very good or very bad with the correlation between the groupings being very high.

46% of schools have a capitation for the careers department of less than £200.

21% of schools have a capitation for the careers department of more than £400.

There are two distinct variations to the second statement. The figure for independent schools is considerably higher at 34% and for Wales considerably lower at 8%.

13% of schools have their capitation for the careers department supplemented by other departments and 38% are supplemented from a 'central pool'. With both sets of figures there is little variation across the groupings.

3.2 With regard to physical resources for careers work such as classrooms, storage space etc, there is very little difference across the groupings. What differences there are, are quite marginal. One anomolous situation which is apparent is that schools are more likely to have an external telephone line than an internal one.

TVEI schools seem to be marginally better off in almost all cases. Schools in Wales also seem to have better physical resources, particularly telephones.

3.3 The schools in the Survey have careers departments which have access to a whole range of equipment, even if the department does not have the exclusive use of that equipment. Very few careers departments reported equipment as 'not available'. The one exception to this being micro computers, where

16% of all careers departments do not have access to a 'micro'.

Careers departments in TVEI schools were only marginally better off, at 13%.

There is a high degree of correlation between the groups, and few great surprises, regarding the extent to which the equipment is used. One exception, surprising for 1986, is that **38% of careers departments never use a 'micro'.**

3.4 **16% of schools subscribe to Prestel and 12% to TTNS.**

Apart from TVEI schools there is little variation in these figures except for independent schools (27% subscribe to Prestel) and metropolitan boroughs (26% subscribe to Prestel). In Scotland 23% of schools subscribe to Prestel. However,

40% of TVEI schools subscribe to Prestel and 27% to TTNS.

3.5 There is moderate variation in the various groupings about the accessibility of the careers information area with only

42% of schools having a careers information area totally accessible to students.

80% of schools provide all students with instruction on the systematic use of careers information.

This is little or no variation in this second figure.

4 THE ORGANISATION OF CAREERS EDUCATION

Section 4 of the questionnaire was concerned with the involvement of particular year groups in careers education (4.1); the amount of time allocated to careers education (4.2); and the status it was accorded in the curriculum (4.3).

4.1 The Survey shows that, overall, some curriculum time is allocated to careers education in years one and two, but not in Wales and not in London in year one. There are some minor variations across the groups, but the Survey does reveal that even in 1986 not all schools see the importance of careers education for all pupils.

31% of schools do not provide careers education for all third year students.

16% of schools do not provide careers education for all fourth year students.

15% of schools do not provide careers education for all fifth year students.

47% of schools do not provide careers education for all sixth formers.

The allocation of time for careers education in TVEI schools in years three, four, five and six is no better than in non-TVEI schools.

4.2 Where time exists for careers education in the various year groups there appears to be little or no variation in the quantity of time allocated. Close examination of the figures shows that, in reality, very little time is allocated.

78% of schools allocate less than 20 hours per year of the third year curriculum time for careers education.

66% of schools allocate less than 20 hours per year of the fourth year curriculum time for careers education.

63% of schools allocate less than 20 hours per year of the fifth year curriculum time for careers education.

81% of schools allocate less than 20 hours per year of the sixth form curriculum time for careers education.

In other words there is less than half an hour per week of careers education for the majority of students.

4.3 The Survey shows that the trend is for careers education to be subsumed in 'social and personal education', although there is considerable variation in the extent to which this has happened.

In 52% of schools careers education is part of social and personal education.

5 TIME

The major part of Section 5 of the Survey questionnaire was concerned with the allocation of time eg how much non-teaching time is allocated (5.1); how heads of careers spend their time (5.2); how much of their own time the head of careers gives to the department (5.3). The availability of clerical help (5.4) and questions relating to record systems, profiling and 'options' (5.5) are also included in this section.

5.1 (a) The amount of non-teaching time allocated to the head of careers (who in 83% of schools is considered to be a head of department) is universally very poor with little or no variation across the groupings.

63% of heads of careers have up to six hours per week of non-teaching time.

(b) When this is analysed for the amount of non-teaching time specifically allocated to careers we find that

62% of heads of careers (not necessarily the same people as in 5.1 (a)) have up to six hours per week of non-teaching time specifically allocated for careers work.

There is little or no variation in this figure across the groupings.

(c) The total amount of non-teaching time which a school allocates specifically for careers is universally very small.

67% of schools allocate up to five hours per week of non-teaching time for careers.

5.2 There are some slight variations across the groupings as to how the head of careers spends his/her time. However, it is clear that, whichever grouping is looked at, the head of careers spends a relatively small amount of time on each of a large range of tasks - up to 10% on all 11 tasks. One alarming trend, however, is that

61% of heads of careers spend more than 25% of their time on non-careers activities.

Although in Wales and TVEI schools this figure is less, in independent schools it is considerably higher.

5.3 Heads of careers are exceedingly generous in the amount of their own time they give to the careers department and it must be remembered that the Survey was taken in the middle of a major industrial dispute in education.

On average, a head of careers gives 6.7 hours of his/her own time to the careers department each week.

In Scotland the figure is much lower, but in London and Wales it is higher. There is, however, little variation across the groupings.

5.4 **In 74% of schools clerical help is available to the careers department, but in only 7% of these schools is a specific amount of time allocated to careers.**

This means that 26% of careers departments have no clerical help available. However, in London this figure is as high as 40%. Elsewhere there is little difference.

In 78% of those schools where a specific amount of time is made available to the careers department, this is less than five hours per week.

5.5 Information about student record systems provides some interesting facts which are fairly consistent across all the groupings. It is intriguing to note that

19% of careers departments do not give the careers service open access to the department's own 'student record system'

7% of careers departments do not have access to their school's 'student record system', and

56% of schools do not give the careers service access to their 'student record system'.

Of the schools participating in the Survey, 33% have a pupil profile system with 34% of the careers departments having a major involvement in the profile. Of the TVEI schools 54% have a pupil profile system, but only 25% of the careers departments have a major involvement.

94% of the schools in the Survey have a 'third year options' system and 65% of the careers departments claim to have a major involvement in the system. There is little variation in the figures across the groupings.

51% of careers departments produce a booklet or provide other information on the occupational significance of choosing particular subjects.

This is a fairly consistent figure across all the groupings.

6 EXTERNAL FACTORS

Section 6 of the Survey questionnaire contained questions which related to factors outside the school's careers department. Questions about careers associations (6.1); the careers service (6.2); employers (6.3); further education (6.4); higher education (6.5); parents (6.6); and former pupils (6.7) were included in this section.

6.1 74% of the respondents had a local careers association, with 42% attending regularly. Although there are some variations across the groupings the only one which varies significantly from the others is Scotland.

The three main activities in which associations engage are:
- liaison with the careers service
- topical discussions
- visits to industry/commerce/FE.

6.2 (a) 5% of the schools in the Survey claim not to have a careers officer working in the school on a regular basis. This figure is probably a distortion caused by the high number of independent schools which feature in this category. However, it must be stated that the same thing applies in 3% of London schools and 1% of TVEI schools. The norm, however, appears to be one or two careers officers working in each school.

(b) **57% of schools have an average of up to five hours each week of careers officer time.**

This is fairly consistent across the groupings except for the independent schools (96%). Despite the extra funding which TVEI has brought to many careers services there is no greater allocation of careers officer time to schools than in non-TVEI schools.

(c) **84% of careers officers spend over 50% of their time in schools interviewing individual students.**

56% of careers officers spend up to 10% of their time in schools interviewing groups of students.

60% of careers officers spend up to 10% of their time in schools helping with third year options.

These are some of the findings of the Survey as regards the way in which a careers officer's 'school time' is allocated.

However, given that schools only receive a very small allocation of careers officer time (see 6.2 (b)) the amount of time which careers officers give to the above tasks is very small indeed.

(d) The analysis of the frequency with which school visits are made by members of the careers service other than the careers officer(s) allocated to the school is very revealing. It shows, for example, that

only 2% of schools are visited regularly by the head of the careers service;

67% of schools never receive a visit from the careers service information officer.

These figures are very consistent across all the groupings.

(e) 74% of schools have a careers officer located in the same town as the school.

Any variations in responses to this question are presumably geographical rather than a case of policy. The exception here is the 2% of all schools in the Survey which have a careers office on site.

(f) The other activities/services which the careers services provide for schools are fairly standard across all the groupings.

6.3 A whole range of questions was asked in this section about the school's links with employers and the extent to which such links are used.

There is a high degree of correlation between the responses to individual questions across the various groupings. It is, however, interesting to note just one or two points.

82% of schools claim that contact with employers is mainly through the careers department.

64% of schools have a policy of ensuring that work experience is 'open and available to all students'.

There is little variation across the groupings in the number of employers with which the careers department has contact.

60% of careers departments have contact with up to 20 employers each year (excluding work experience).

On average, TVEI schools appear to have contact with a larger number of employers.

6.4 There is a high degree of consistency as to the way in which students are informed about further education courses. However, there does not appear to be very much contact between the staff of schools and the staff at further education colleges.

9% of schools have regular meetings between the school staff and the FE college staff.

6.5 There is also a similar consistency about the way in which students are informed about higher education.

6.6 There is very little variation in the way in which the school's careers department communicates with parents. However, in Scotland it does appear that more is left to chance than in any of the other groupings.

Again the degree to which parents are used in the careers process is very similar, except in independent schools where it is very high and in Wales where it is very low.

6.7 **67% of schools attempt to use the experience of former students in the careers process.**

This is fairly consistent across the groupings except for independent schools where the figure is much higher at 87%. The methods used are also fairly consistent, with specific invitations to individuals being the most common.

56% of schools making use of former students write specific invitations to individuals inviting them back to school for this purpose.

This page has been intentionally left blank

IV THE ANALYSIS

LIST OF GRAPHS AND TABLES

The following pages contain graphs and tables produced using statistics gathered from the Survey. The numbers on the left-hand side of the list refer to the paragraph numbers originally used in the Survey questionnaire - please refer to Appendix 2.

		Page
1.1	Size of the schools	24
1.2	Age range of students	26
1.3	Designation of the schools	28
1.4	Catchment area of schools	30
1.5 - 1.10	Careers education in school and LEA	32
2.1	Number of teachers involved in careers	33
2.2 - 2.8	Status etc of careers teachers	34
2.9	Training undertaken by careers teachers	36
3.1	Finance available to careers departments	37
3.2 - 3.6	Resources available to careers departments	38
3.3	Equipment available to careers departments	40
4.1	Organisation of classroom careers work	42
4.2	Curriculum time allocated to careers	44
4.3	Careers as a curricular subject	46
5.1	Non-teaching time allocated to head of careers and its use	48
5.2 - 5.4	Principal activities of heads of careers	54
5.5 - 5.8	Record, profile and options systems	58
6.1	Attendance and activities of careers associations	59
6.2	School's contact with careers service	60
6.3	School's contact with employers	70
6.4(b)	Methods of informing students about further education courses	74
6.4(c)	Frequency of meetings between school and college staff	76
6.5(b)	Methods of informing students about higher education	78
6.6(a)	Careers department's contact with parents	80
6.6(b)	Involvement of parents in the careers process	82
6.7	Involvement of former students in the careers process	84

NOTE: the scales used for the bar charts vary depending on the size of the figures involved. In making comparisons between the charts on one spread please use the figures provided.

1.1 Size of the schools

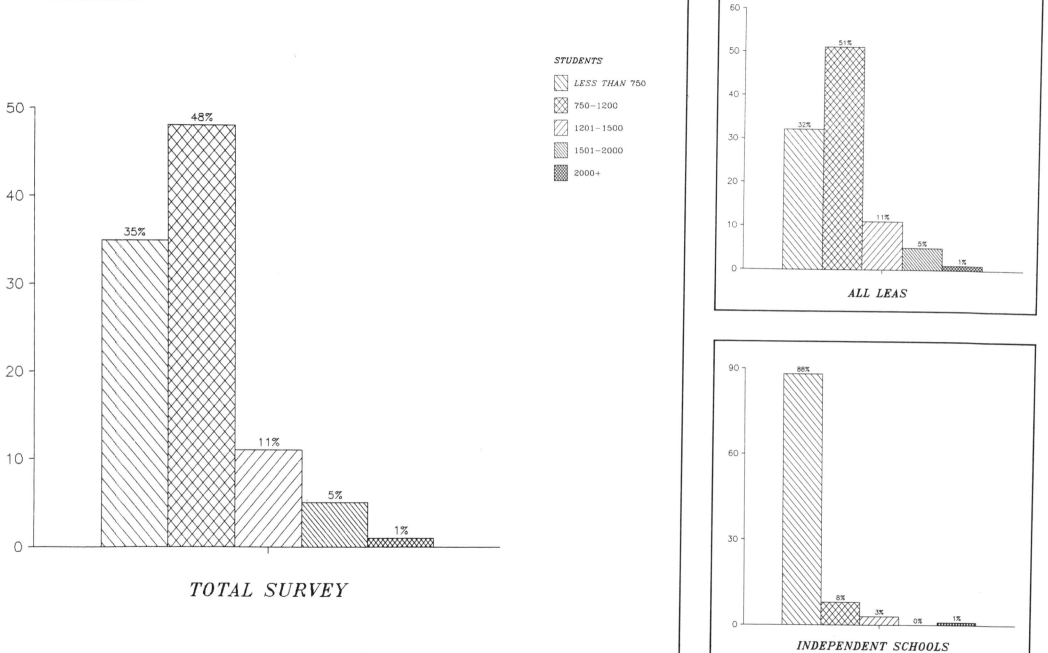

STUDENTS

- LESS THAN 750
- 750–1200
- 1201–1500
- 1501–2000
- 2000+

TOTAL SURVEY

ALL LEAS

INDEPENDENT SCHOOLS

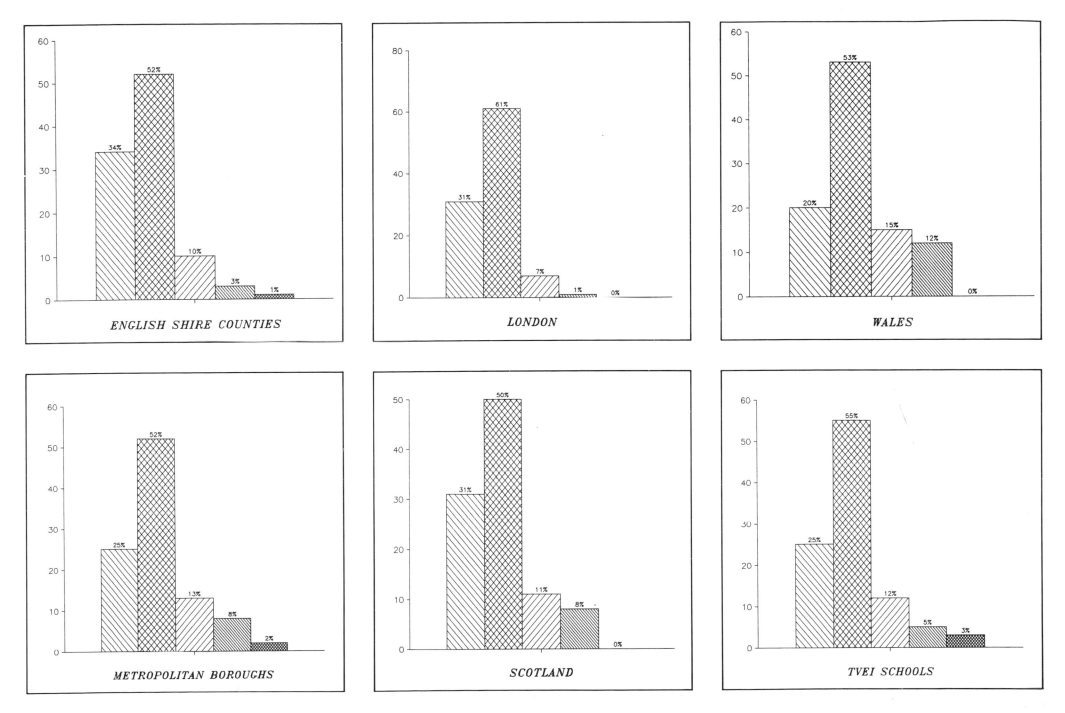

ENGLISH SHIRE COUNTIES

LONDON

WALES

METROPOLITAN BOROUGHS

SCOTLAND

TVEI SCHOOLS

1.2 Age range of students

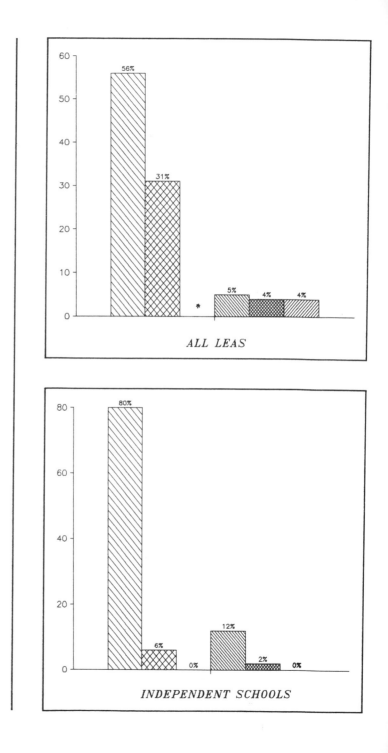

ALL LEAS

INDEPENDENT SCHOOLS

Legend:
- 11 (OR 12) −18 YRS
- 11 (OR 12) −16 YRS
- 11−14 YRS
- 13−18 YRS
- 14−18 YRS
- 16+ YRS

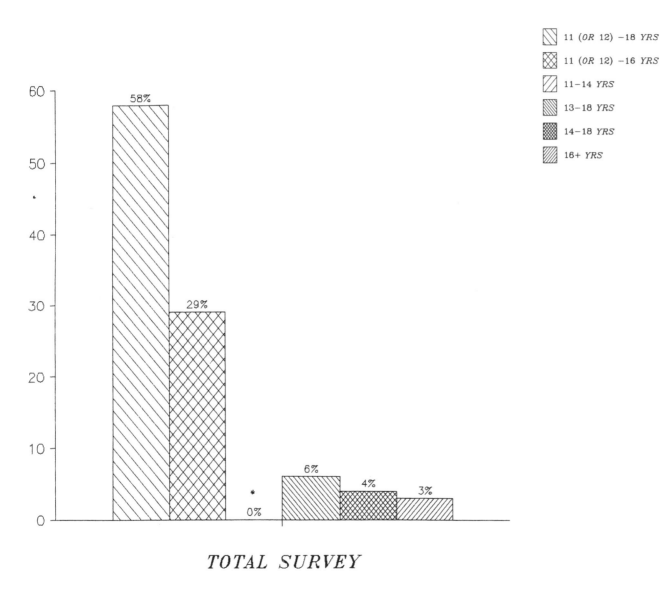

TOTAL SURVEY

*   *One school in the survey was in the age range.*

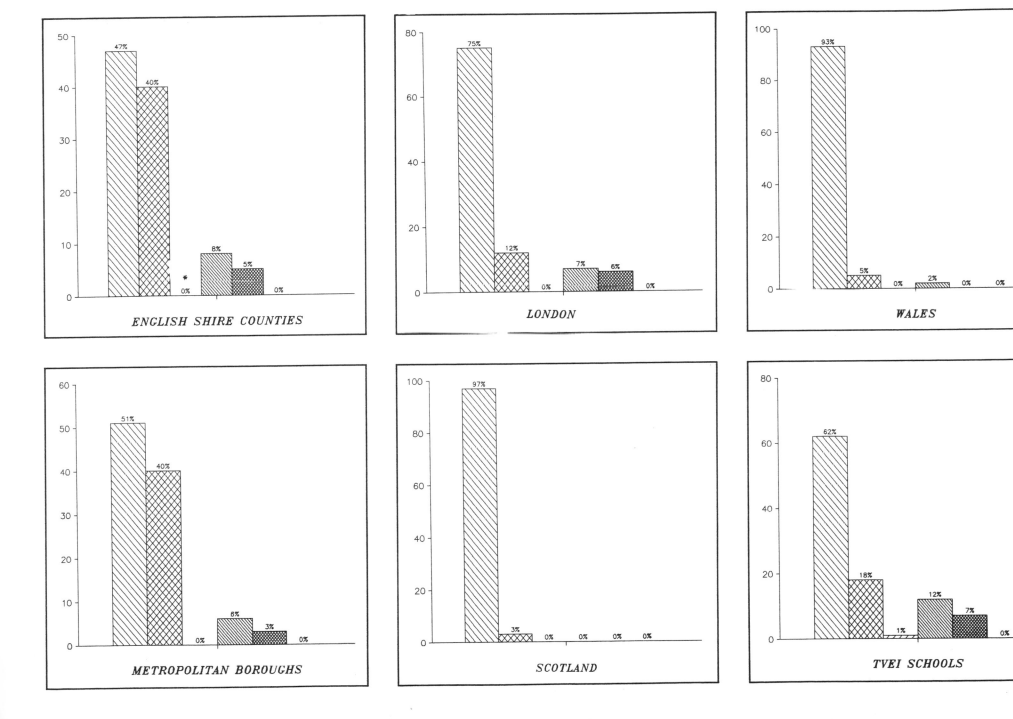

ENGLISH SHIRE COUNTIES

LONDON

WALES

METROPOLITAN BOROUGHS

SCOTLAND

TVEI SCHOOLS

1.3 Designation of the schools

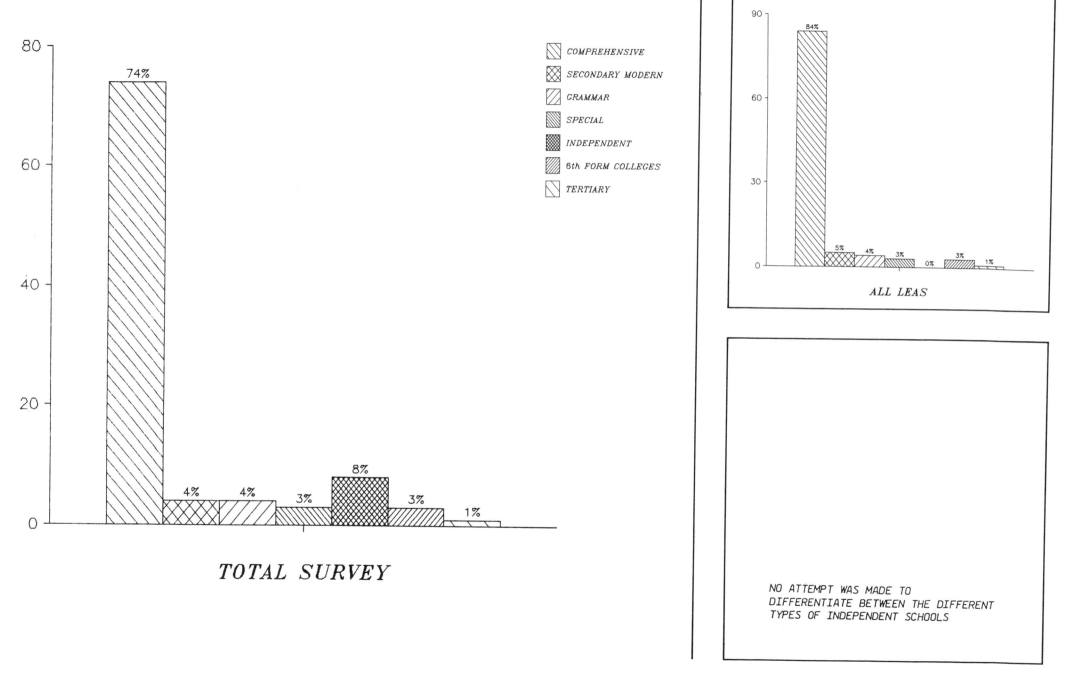

COMPREHENSIVE
SECONDARY MODERN
GRAMMAR
SPECIAL
INDEPENDENT
6th FORM COLLEGES
TERTIARY

74%

4%   4%   3%   8%   3%   1%

TOTAL SURVEY

84%

5% 4% 3% 0% 3% 1%

ALL LEAS

NO ATTEMPT WAS MADE TO
DIFFERENTIATE BETWEEN THE DIFFERENT
TYPES OF INDEPENDENT SCHOOLS

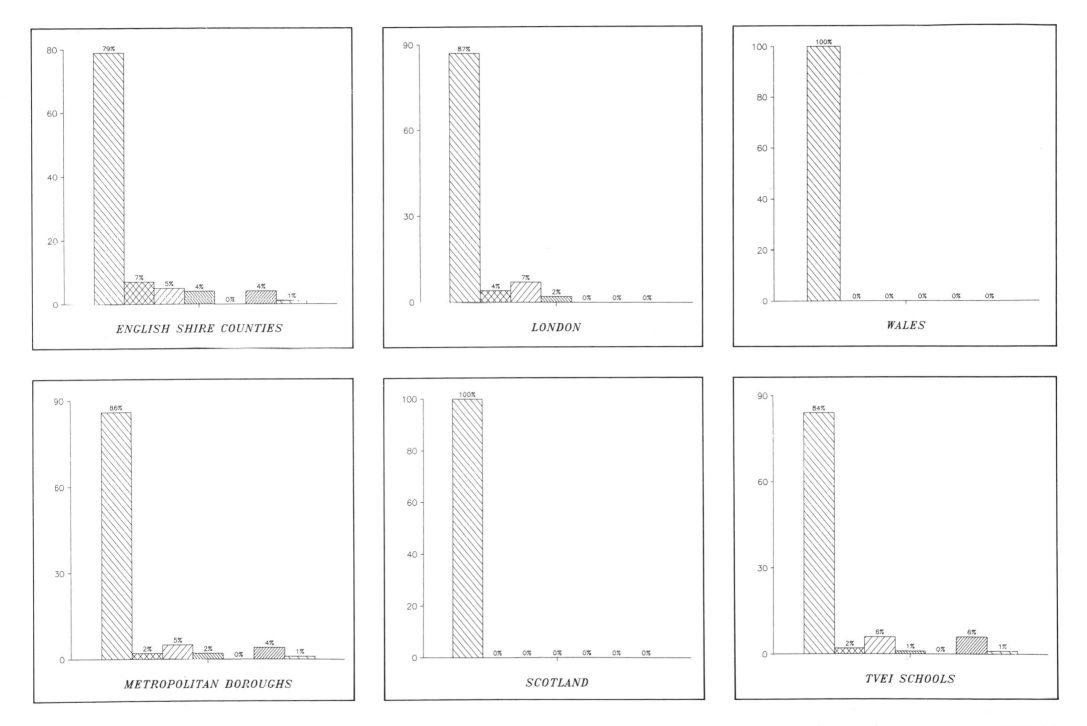

ENGLISH SHIRE COUNTIES

LONDON

WALES

METROPOLITAN BOROUGHS

SCOTLAND

TVEI SCHOOLS

1.4 Catchment area of schools

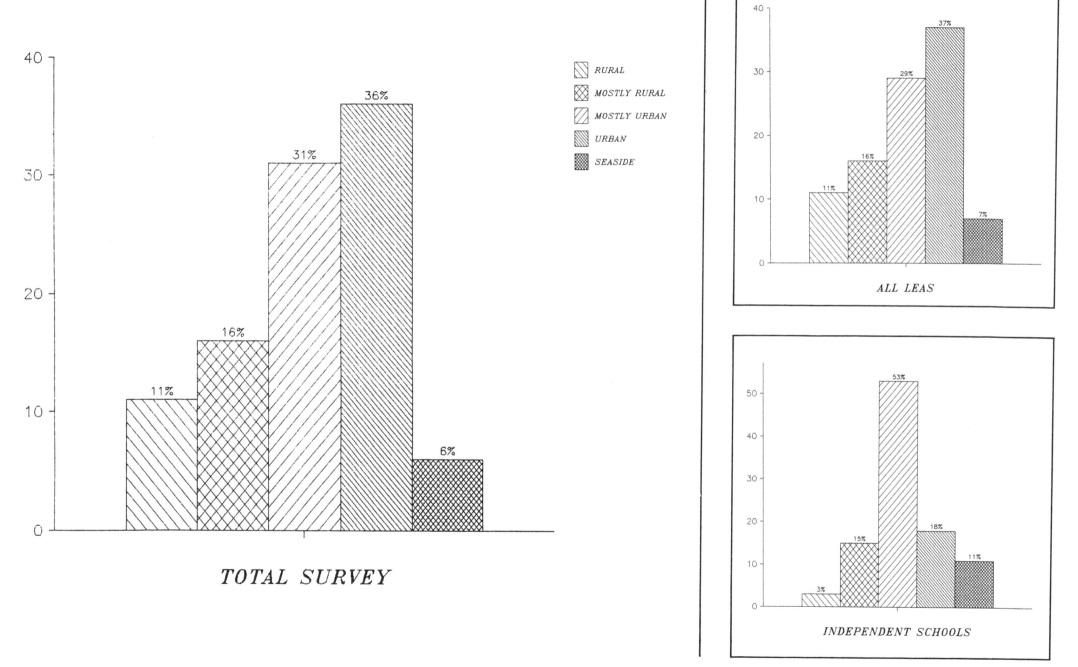

RURAL

MOSTLY RURAL

MOSTLY URBAN

URBAN

SEASIDE

TOTAL SURVEY

ALL LEAS

INDEPENDENT SCHOOLS

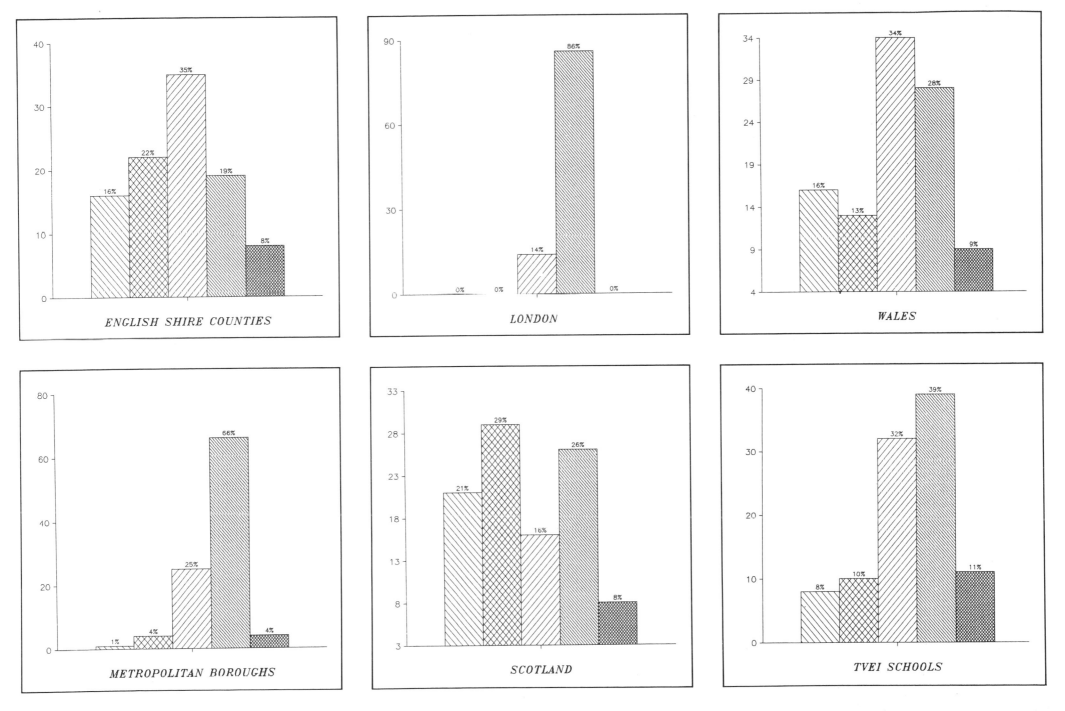

ENGLISH SHIRE COUNTIES

LONDON

WALES

METROPOLITAN BOROUGHS

SCOTLAND

TVEI SCHOOLS

		TOTAL SURVEY	ALL LEAS	INDEP SCHOOLS	SHIRE COUNTIES	METRO BOROUGHS	LONDON	SCOTLAND	WALES	TVEI SCHOOLS
1.5 DOES THE SCHOOL PARTICIPATE IN TVEI?	YES	16%	17%	0%	15%	21%	21%	24%	26%	100%
	NO	84%	83%	100%	85%	79%	79%	76%	74%	—
1.6 DOES THE SCHOOL PROVIDE CPVE COURSES?	YES	38%	41%	3%	38%	37%	54%	15%	68%	58%
	NO	62%	59%	97%	62%	63%	46%	85%	32%	42%
1.7 DOES THE SCHOOL HAVE A WRITTEN POLICY FOR CAREERS EDUCATION?	YES	71%	73%	49%	74%	81%	58%	56%	76%	77%
	NO	26%	24%	46%	24%	16%	31%	41%	24%	20%
	DON'T KNOW	3%	3%	5%	2%	3%	11%	3%	0%	3%
1.9 DOES THE LEA HAVE A WRITTEN POLICY FOR CAREERS EDUCATION?	YES	52%	52%	—	54%	38%	53%	41%	41%	45%
	NO	12%	12%	—	11%	17%	14%	16%	28%	20%
	DON'T KNOW	36%	36%	—	35%	45%	33%	44%	31%	35%
1.10 IS THERE AN LEA ADVISER/INSPECTOR FOR CAREERS EDUCATION?	YES	59%	59%	—	58%	45%	68%	56%	55%	47%
	NO	29%	30%	—	30%	38%	25%	35%	38%	38%
	DON'T KNOW	12%	11%	—	12%	17%	7%	9%	7%	15%
IS THIS SHARED WITH ANOTHER SUBJECT?	YES	51%	51%	—	49%	67%	66%	74%	78%	65%
	NO	49%	49%	—	51%	33%	34%	26%	22%	35%

2.1 HOW MANY TEACHERS ARE FORMALLY INVOLVED IN CAREERS WORK?	TOTAL SURVEY	ALL LEAS	INDEP SCHOOLS	SHIRE COUNTIES	METRO BOROUGHS	LONDON	SCOTLAND	WALES	TVEI SCHOOLS
1	22%	21%	33%	23%	20%	18%	13%	21%	21%
2	23%	24%	20%	21%	19%	37%	9%	28%	17%
3	12%	11%	14%	12%	9%	18%	4%	12%	11%
4	10%	10%	16%	10%	7%	8%	9%	14%	9%
5	7%	7%	4%	8%	8%	3%	4%	7%	8%
6	5%	5%	2%	6%	3%	7%	——	2%	7%
7	3%	3%	2%	3%	4%	3%	9%	7%	4%
8	5%	5%	3%	4%	5%	1%	15%	7%	9%
9	1%	1%	4%	1%	1%	1%	2%	——	1%
10	1%	1%	——	1%	3%	——	2%	——	4%
10+	11%	12%	——	11%	19%	4%	33%	2%	9%

		TOTAL SURVEY	ALL LEAS	INDEP SCHOOLS	SHIRE COUNTIES	METRO BOROUGHS	LONDON	SCOTLAND	WALES	TVEI SCHOOLS
2.2	% DESIGNATED CAREERS TEACHERS	70%	76%	16%	89%	67%	60%	28%	52%	61%
2.3	% MEMBERS OF NACGT	24%	24%	22%	28%	24%	22%	2%	22%	31%
2.4	% PAID ALLOWANCE FOR CAREERS WORK	53%	59%	38%	60%	53%	60%	59%	24%	51%
2.5 SALARY SCALE OF SENIOR CAREERS TEACHER (DOES NOT INCLUDE SCOTLAND)	I	2%	1%	9%	1%	1%	1%	20%	—	1%
	II	11%	10%	26%	11%	11%	10%	—	3%	5%
	III	45%	45%	33%	46%	43%	43%	—	54%	40%
	IV	29%	30%	20%	29%	31%	31%	ASST PRIN 10%	31%	36%
	SENIOR TEACHER	9%	9%	8%	8%	10%	13%	PRINCIPAL TEACHER 50%	8%	14%
	DEPUTY HEAD	4%	5%	4%	5%	4%	2%	ASST HEAD 20%	4%	4%
PURELY FOR CAREERS WORK?	YES	36%	37%	29%	37%	39%	31%	18%	32%	39%
	NO	64%	63%	71%	63%	61%	69%	82%	68%	61%
2.6 IS THE SENIOR TEACHER A HEAD OF DEPARTMENT?	YES	83%	80%	78%	83%	84%	88%	48%	84%	85%
	NO	17%	20%	22%	17%	16%	12%	52%	16%	14%

		TOTAL SURVEY	ALL LEAS	INDEP SCHOOLS	SHIRE COUNTIES	METRO BOROUGHS	LONDON	SCOTLAND	WALES	TVEI SCHOOLS
2.7 DOES THE HEAD OF CAREERS PARTICIPATE IN SCHOOL MANAGEMENT DECISIONS?	ALWAYS	16%	16%	14%	17%	16%	16%	26%	16%	16%
	USUALLY	36%	36%	44%	37%	31%	40%	19%	30%	42%
	RARELY	30%	31%	24%	31%	34%	26%	26%	28%	26%
	NEVER	18%	17%	18%	15%	19%	18%	29%	26%	16%
DOES THE HEAD OF CAREERS SIT ON THE SCHOOL'S CURRICULUM COMMITTEE?	ALWAYS	37%	36%	33%	39%	34%	37%	23%	30%	40%
	USUALLY	26%	27%	23%	28%	27%	29%	15%	18%	31%
	RARELY	12%	12%	13%	12%	10%	15%	12%	17%	9%
	NEVER	25%	25%	31%	21%	29%	19%	50%	35%	20%
2.8 EQUIVALENT NUMBER OF FULL TIME CAREERS TEACHERS	LESS THAN 1	60%	58%	78%	61%	47%	67%	79%	70%	46%
	BETWEEN 1 AND 2	35%	37%	20%	33%	48%	30%	18%	30%	47%
	BETWEEN 2 AND 3	3%	3%	——	4%	3%	3%	——	——	5%
	BETWEEN 3 AND 4	1%	1%	——	1%	1%	——	——	——	1%
	MORE THAN 4	1%	1%	2%	1%	1%	——	3%	——	1%

2.9 HOW MUCH TRAINING HAVE THE DESIGNATED CAREERS TEACHERS HAD ?	TOTAL SURVEY	ALL LEAS	INDEP SCHOOLS	SHIRE COUNTIES	METRO BOROUGHS	LONDON	SCOTLAND	WALES	TVEI SCHOOLS
LESS THAN 5 DAYS	41%	40%	50%	37%	39%	49%	42%	50%	32%
BETWEEN 5 AND 20 DAYS	27%	27%	35%	28%	23%	28%	27%	20%	28%
BETWEEN 21 AND 50 DAYS	15%	15%	7%	16%	12%	9%	20%	22%	22%
A F/T COURSE OF 1 TERM	3%	3%	2%	4%	3%	1%	—	—	2%
A F/T COURSE OF 1 YEAR	4%	4%	1%	4%	8%	2%	—	4%	5%
A P/T COURSE OF LESS THAN 1 YEAR	3%	3%	2%	3%	6%	2%	3%	2%	2%
A P/T COURSE OF AT LEAST 1 YEAR	7%	8%	3%	8%	9%	9%	8%	2%	9%

3.1 HOW MUCH FINANCE FOR THE CAREERS DEPT ?		TOTAL SURVEY	ALL LEAS	INDEP SCHOOLS	SHIRE COUNTIES	METRO BOROUGHS	LONDON	SCOTLAND	WALES	TVEI SCHOOLS
UP TO #50		5%	5%	8%	5%	7%	3%	13%	7%	4%
BETWEEN #51-#100		11%	12%	2%	12%	10%	4%	16%	21%	11%
BETWEEN #101-#150		12%	12%	13%	13%	13%	7%	20%	19%	15%
BETWEEN #151-#200		18%	16%	20%	16%	19%	11%	26%	17%	14%
BETWEEN #201-#250		11%	12%	4%	11%	8%	21%	——	12%	7%
BETWEEN #251-#300		8%	9%	4%	9%	9%	9%	3%	12%	10%
BETWEEN #301-#350		7%	7%	7%	7%	9%	10%	3%	2%	7%
BETWEEN #351-#400		7%	7%	8%	7%	7%	14%	3%	2%	8%
MORE THAN #400		21%	20%	34%	20%	18%	21%	16%	8%	24%
IN THIS SUPPLEMENTED BY HELP FROM OTHER DEPT ?	YES	13%	13%	7%	14%	14%	7%	13%	6%	17%
	NO	87%	87%	93%	86%	86%	93%	87%	94%	83%
OR HELP FROM CENTRAL POOL ?	YES	38%	37%	37%	39%	42%	24%	42%	36%	33%
	NO	62%	63%	63%	61%	58%	76%	58%	74%	67%

POUND SIGN

3.2 DOES THE CAREERS DEPT HAVE THE FOLLOWING ?	TOTAL SURVEY	ALL LEAS	INDEP SCHOOLS	SHIRE COUNTIES	METRO BOROUGHS	LONDON	SCOTLAND	WALES	TVEI SCHOOLS
A CAREERS CLASSROOM	44%	45%	28%	40%	60%	55%	15%	47%	51%
A SEPARATE OFFICE FOR HOD	69%	71%	48%	76%	68%	68%	33%	80%	82%
AN INTERVIEW ROOM	68%	68%	67%	69%	66%	63%	71%	88%	76%
STORAGE SPACE	84%	83%	89%	84%	80%	87%	80%	83%	87%
A CAREERS DISPLAY AREA	88%	87%	97%	89%	86%	86%	100%	82%	93%
A SEPARATE CAREERS LIBRARY	68%	66%	81%	71%	58%	72%	74%	40%	65%
A DISPLAY AREA FOR VACANCIES AND YTS	70%	83%	51%	85%	80%	81%	88%	84%	92%
AN EXTERNAL TELEPHONE LINE	68%	69%	46%	67%	65%	70%	69%	80%	76%
AN INTERNAL TELEPHONE LINE	66%	67%	46%	66%	59%	74%	69%	73%	71%

	TOTAL SURVEY	ALL LEAS	INDEP SCHOOLS	SHIRE COUNTIES	METRO BOROUGHS	LONDON	SCOTLAND	WALES	TVEI SCHOOLS
3.4 SCHOOLS SUBSCRIBING TO PRESTEL	16%	16%	27%	14%	26%	18%	23%	9%	40%
SCHOOLS SUBSCRIBING TO TTNS	12%	12%	11%	11%	17%	15%	10%	13%	27%
3.5 IS THE CAREERS INFORMATION AREA: TOTALLY ACCESSIBLE?	42%	40%	66%	43%	29%	39%	45%	39%	45%
AVAILABLE AT CERTAIN TIMES?	53%	54%	30%	52%	60%	60%	55%	51%	52%
ONLY ON REQUEST?	5%	6%	4%	5%	11%	1%	——	10%	3%
3.6 INSTRUCTION FOR ALL STUDENTS IN THE SYSTEMATIC USE OF CAREERS INFORMATION	80%	80%	76%	84%	77%	82%	78%	63%	81%

3.3 WHAT EQUIPMENT IS AVAILABLE ?		TOTAL SURVEY	ALL LEAS	INDEP SCHOOLS	SHIRE COUNTIES	METRO BOROUGHS	LONDON	SCOTLAND	WALES	TVEI SCHOOLS
RADIO	EXCLUSIVELY BY CAREERS	13%	13%	8%	13%	17%	20%	7%	11%	15%
	AVAILABLE	79%	79%	84%	80%	76%	76%	71%	81%	78%
	NOT AVAILABLE	8%	8%	8%	7%	7%	4%	22%	8%	7%
T.V.	EXCLUSIVELY BY CAREERS	13%	13%	5%	15%	11%	13%	3%	22%	17%
	AVAILABLE	86%	86%	92%	84%	88%	87%	97%	78%	83%
	NOT AVAILABLE	1%	1%	3%	1%	1%	—	—	—	—
VIDEO	EXCLUSIVELY BY CAREERS	11%	12%	5%	11%	10%	11%	3%	21%	19%
	AVAILABLE	88%	87%	90%	88%	87%	88%	94%	77%	81%
	NOT AVAILABLE	1%	1%	5%	1%	3%	1%	3%	2%	—
OVERHEAD PROJECTOR	EXCLUSIVELY BY CAREERS	16%	17%	7%	16%	16%	29%	3%	25%	21%
	AVAILABLE	80%	80%	88%	82%	79%	66%	94%	71%	76%
	NOT AVAILABLE	4%	3%	5%	2%	5%	5%	3%	4%	3%
MICRO	EXCLUSIVELY BY CAREERS	12%	11%	29%	12%	9%	14%	—	5%	20%
	AVAILABLE	72%	73%	60%	73%	74%	72%	87%	64%	67%
	NOT AVAILABLE	16%	16%	11%	15%	17%	14%	13%	31%	13%
FILM PROJECTOR	EXCLUSIVELY BY CAREERS	5%	5%	—	4%	5%	10%	—	10%	7%
	AVAILABLE	92%	92%	91%	92%	92%	88%	100%	86%	89%
	NOT AVAILABLE	3%	3%	9%	4%	3%	2%	—	4%	4%

TO WHAT EXTENT IS IT USED ?		TOTAL SURVEY	ALL LEAS	INDEP SCHOOLS	SHIRE COUNTIES	METRO BOROUGHS	LONDON	SCOTLAND	WALES	TVEI SCHOOLS
RADIO	USED REGULARLY	5%	5%	——	5%	8%	7%	——	6%	12%
	USED	38%	39%	32%	38%	41%	32%	37%	53%	40%
	NEVER USED	57%	56%	68%	57%	51%	61%	63%	41%	48%
T.V.	USED REGULARLY	56%	58%	35%	57%	54%	58%	54%	55%	62%
	USED	38%	38%	41%	38%	43%	37%	42%	43%	35%
	NEVER USED	6%	4%	24%	5%	3%	5%	4%	2%	3%
VIDEO	USED REGULARLY	63%	64%	52%	65%	58%	64%	69%	59%	67%
	USED	36%	35%	42%	35%	42%	30%	31%	38%	32%
	NEVER USED	1%	1%	6%	——	——	6%	——	3%	1%
OVERHEAD PROJECTOR	USED REGULARLY	21%	22%	13%	23%	20%	23%	——	16%	22%
	USED	60%	60%	51%	59%	57%	54%	95%	66%	66%
	NEVER USED	19%	18%	31%	18%	23%	23%	5%	18%	12%
MICRO	USED REGULARLY	20%	18%	33%	24%	11%	14%	19%	3%	27%
	USED	42%	41%	45%	38%	48%	42%	71%	33%	37%
	NEVER USED	38%	41%	22%	38%	41%	14%	10%	64%	36%
FILM PROJECTOR	USED REGULARLY	14%	14%	10%	17%	11%	4%	12%	24%	20%
	USED	64%	65%	52%	66%	70%	48%	80%	70%	62%
	NEVER USED	22%	21%	38%	17%	19%	48%	8%	6%	18%

4.1 Organisation of classroom careers work

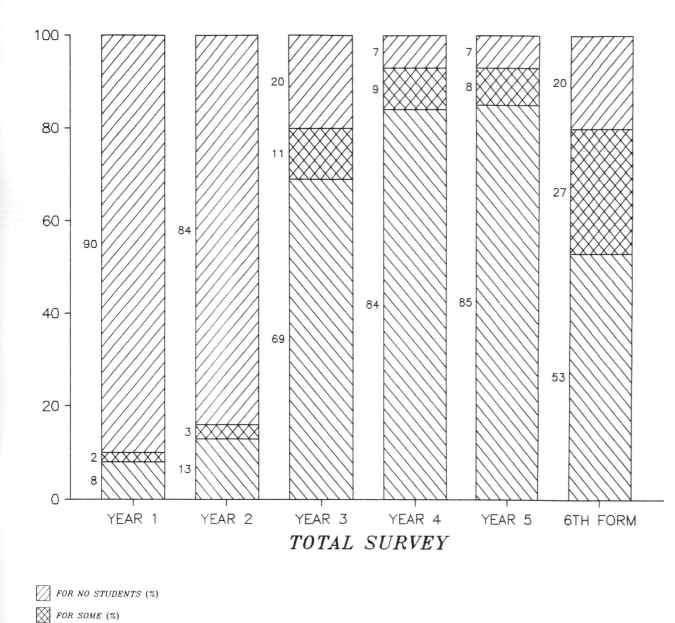

TOTAL SURVEY

⬚ FOR NO STUDENTS (%)

▨ FOR SOME (%)

◩ FOR ALL (%)

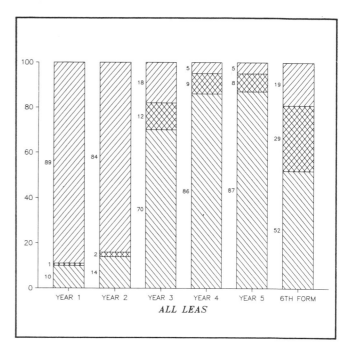

ALL LEAS

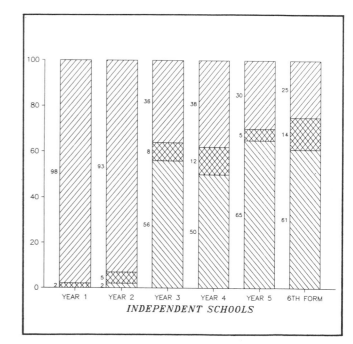

INDEPENDENT SCHOOLS

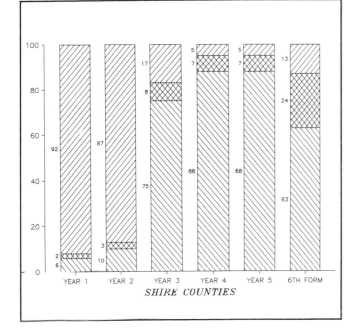

SHIRE COUNTIES

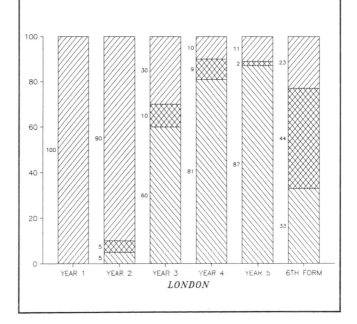

LONDON

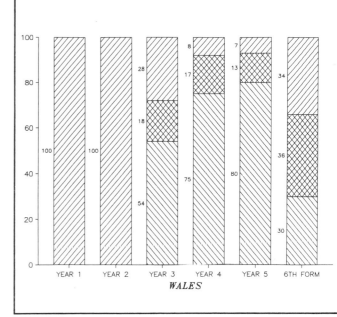

WALES

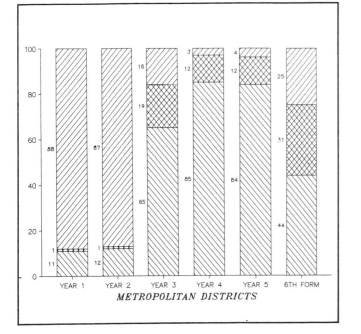

METROPOLITAN DISTRICTS

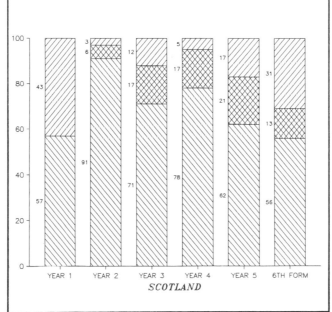

SCOTLAND

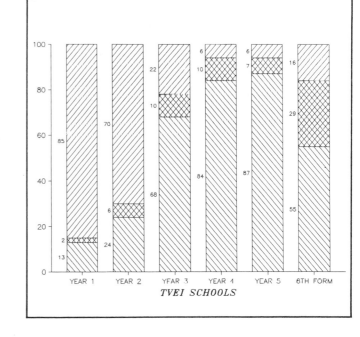

TVEI SCHOOLS

4.2 Curriculum time allocated to careers education per week

	UP TO 10 HOURS	11-20 HOURS	21-30 HOURS	31-40 HOURS	MORE THAN 40 HOURS
YEAR 1	68%	8%	7%	5%	12%
YEAR 2	64%	16%	7%	5%	8%
YEAR 3	53%	25%	16%	4%	2%
YEAR 4	29%	37%	20%	9%	5%
YEAR 5	26%	37%	21%	10%	6%
6TH FORM	53%	28%	11%	5%	3%

TOTAL SURVEY

	UP TO 10 HOURS	11-20 HOURS	21-30 HOURS	31-40 HOURS	MORE THAN 40 HOURS
YEAR 1	69%	7%	7%	6%	11%
YEAR 2	64%	16%	6%	5%	8%
YEAR 3	52%	26%	16%	4%	2%
YEAR 4	27%	38%	21%	9%	5%
YEAR 5	24%	38%	20%	11%	7%
6TH FORM	52%	28%	12%	5%	3%

ALL LEAS

	UP TO 10 HOURS	11-20 HOURS	21-30 HOURS	31-40 HOURS	MORE THAN 40 HOURS
YEAR 1	60%	20%	—	—	20%
YEAR 2	50%	17%	17%	—	16%
YEAR 3	62%	23%	13%	2%	—
YEAR 4	56%	21%	15%	5%	3%
YEAR 5	51%	23%	19%	5%	2%
6TH FORM	53%	25%	9%	11%	2%

INDEPENDENT SCHOOLS

4.4

% OF TOTAL SCHOOLS USING JIIG/CAL = 31%

% OF SCHOOLS IN LEAS USING JIIG/CAL = 32%

% OF SCHOOLS IN SHIRE COUNTIES USING JIIG/CAL = 30%

% OF SCHOOLS IN LONDON USING JIIG/CAL = 46%

% OF SCHOOLS IN WALES USING JIIG/CAL = 21%

% OF INDEPENDENT SCHOOLS USING JIIG/CAL = 13%

% OF METROPOLITAN DISTRICTS USING JIIG/CAL = 26%

% OF SCHOOLS IN SCOTLAND USING JIIG/CAL = 54%

% OF TVEI SCHOOLS USING JIIG/CAL = 39%

SHIRE COUNTIES

	UP TO 10 HOURS	11-20 HOURS	21-30 HOURS	31-40 HOURS	MORE THAN 40 HOURS
YEAR 1	59%	7%	7%	10%	17%
YEAR 2	58%	13%	10%	6%	13%
YEAR 3	53%	28%	11%	6%	2%
YEAR 4	29%	38%	17%	11%	5%
YEAR 5	26%	39%	17%	12%	6%
6TH FORM	56%	28%	12%	2%	2%

LONDON

	UP TO 10 HOURS	11-20 HOURS	21-30 HOURS	31-40 HOURS	MORE THAN 40 HOURS
YEAR 1	—	—	—	—	—
YEAR 2	100%	—	—	—	—
YEAR 3	66%	16%	16%	2%	—
YEAR 4	28%	41%	23%	5%	3%
YEAR 5	20%	40%	26%	8%	6%
6TH FORM	67%	11%	8%	8%	6%

WALES

	UP TO 10 HOURS	11-20 HOURS	21-30 HOURS	31-40 HOURS	MORE THAN 40 HOURS
YEAR 1	—	—	—	—	—
YEAR 2	—	—	—	—	—
YEAR 3	43%	27%	27%	—	3%
YEAR 4	17%	44%	21%	12%	6%
YEAR 5	16%	44%	25%	9%	6%
6TH FORM	50%	32%	11%	7%	—

METROPOLITAN BOROUGHS

	UP TO 10 HOURS	11-20 HOURS	21-30 HOURS	31-40 HOURS	MORE THAN 40 HOURS
YEAR 1	53%	18%	12%	5%	12%
YEAR 2	58%	16%	5%	11%	10%
YEAR 3	40%	30%	22%	4%	4%
YEAR 4	23%	30%	30%	8%	9%
YEAR 5	21%	30%	28%	10%	11%
6TH FORM	40%	35%	19%	3%	3%

SCOTLAND

	UP TO 10 HOURS	11-20 HOURS	21-30 HOURS	31-40 HOURS	MORE THAN 40 HOURS
YEAR 1	100%	—	—	—	—
YEAR 2	77%	23%	—	—	—
YEAR 3	74%	15%	11%	—	—
YEAR 4	56%	31%	13%	—	—
YEAR 5	68%	32%	—	—	—
6TH FORM	78%	22%	—	—	—

TVEI SCHOOLS

	UP TO 10 HOURS	11-20 HOURS	21-30 HOURS	31-40 HOURS	MORE THAN 40 HOURS
YEAR 1	72%	14%	—	14%	—
YEAR 2	71%	8%	8%	13%	—
YEAR 3	48%	27%	15%	8%	2%
YEAR 4	26%	36%	26%	7%	5%
YEAR 5	23%	34%	24%	11%	8%
6TH FORM	50%	26%	18%	4%	2%

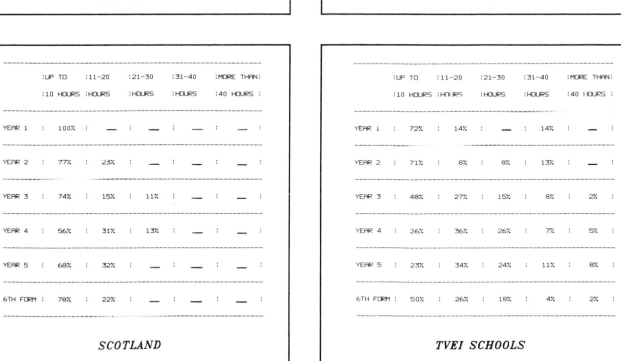

4.3 Does careers education stand as a subject on its own?

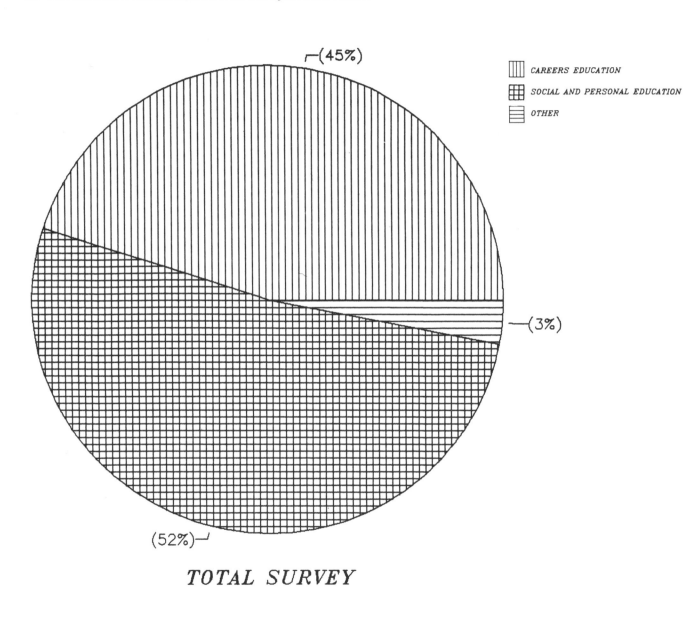

CAREERS EDUCATION

SOCIAL AND PERSONAL EDUCATION

OTHER

(45%)

(3%)

(52%)

TOTAL SURVEY

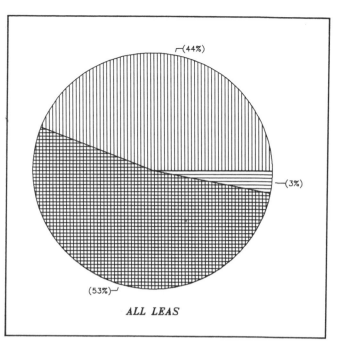

(44%)

(3%)

(53%)

ALL LEAS

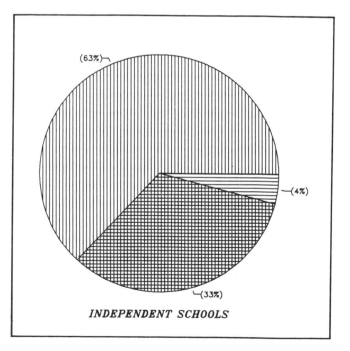

(63%)

(4%)

(33%)

INDEPENDENT SCHOOLS

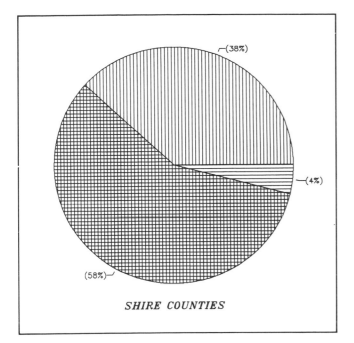

(38%) (4%) (58%)

SHIRE COUNTIES

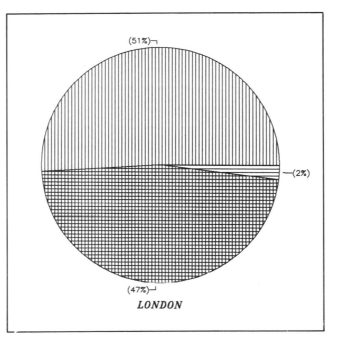

(51%) (2%) (47%)

LONDON

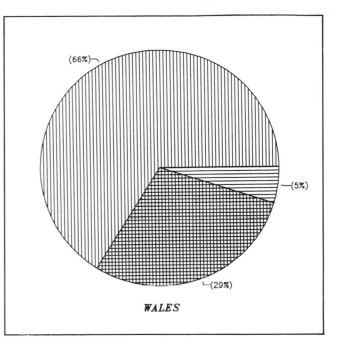

(66%) (5%) (29%)

WALES

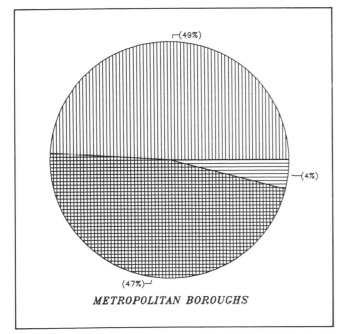

(49%) (4%) (47%)

METROPOLITAN BOROUGHS

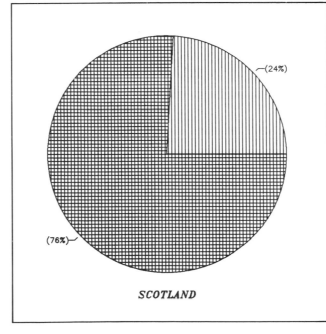

(24%) (76%)

SCOTLAND

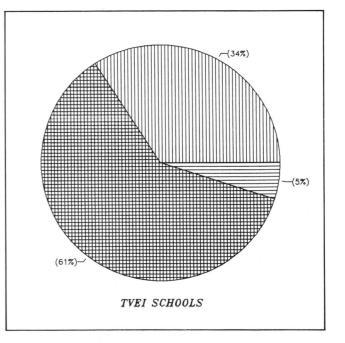

(34%) (5%) (61%)

TVEI SCHOOLS

5.1 (a) How much non-teaching time is allocated to the head of careers?

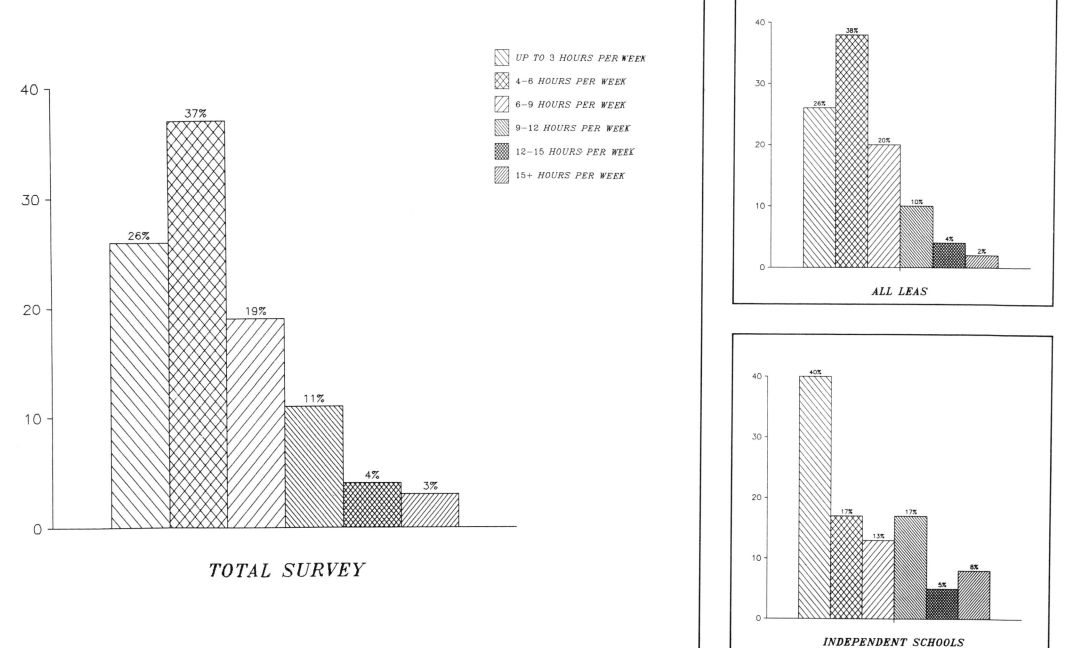

UP TO 3 HOURS PER WEEK
4–6 HOURS PER WEEK
6–9 HOURS PER WEEK
9–12 HOURS PER WEEK
12–15 HOURS PER WEEK
15+ HOURS PER WEEK

TOTAL SURVEY

ALL LEAS

INDEPENDENT SCHOOLS

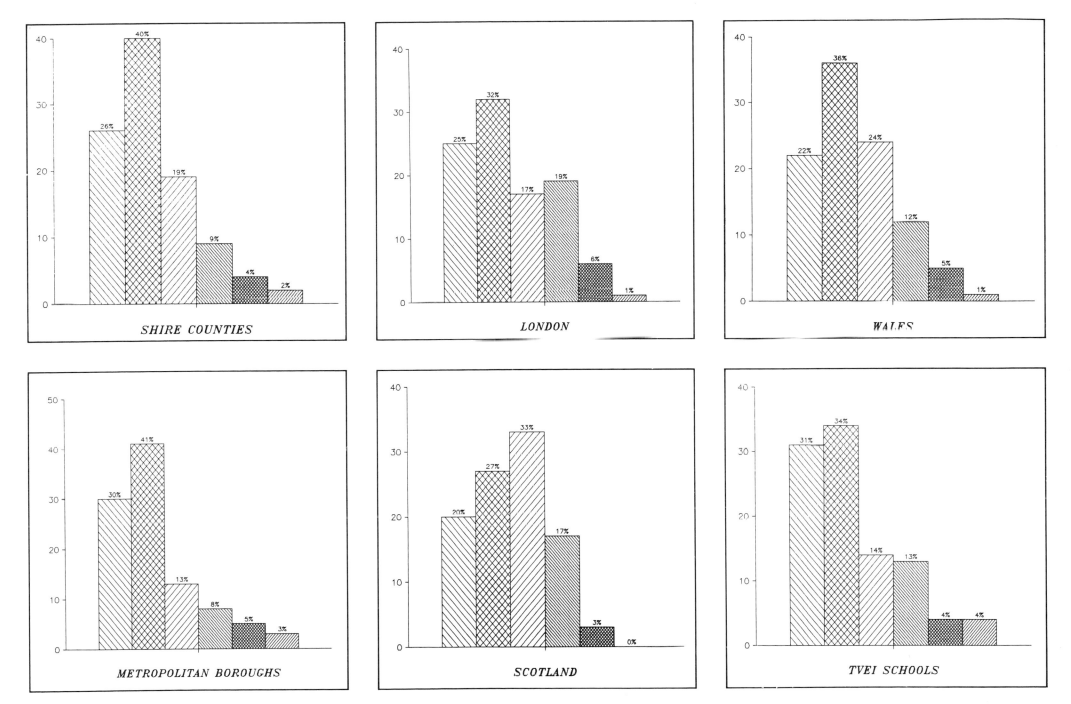

SHIRE COUNTIES

LONDON

WALES

METROPOLITAN BOROUGHS

SCOTLAND

TVEI SCHOOLS

5.1 (b)   How much of this time (5.1.a) is specifically for careers?

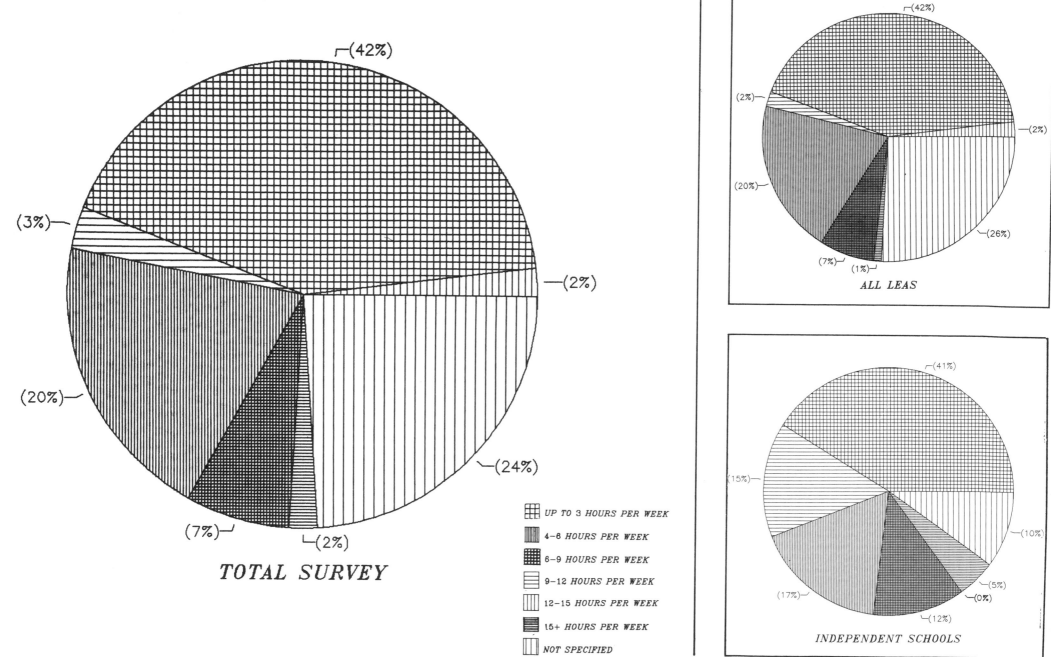

(42%)

(3%)

(2%)

(20%)

(24%)

(7%)

(2%)

TOTAL SURVEY

(42%)

(2%)

(2%)

(20%)

(26%)

(7%) (1%)

ALL LEAS

(41%)

(15%)

(10%)

(17%)

(5%)

(12%)

(0%)

INDEPENDENT SCHOOLS

UP TO 3 HOURS PER WEEK

4–6 HOURS PER WEEK

6–9 HOURS PER WEEK

9–12 HOURS PER WEEK

12–15 HOURS PER WEEK

15+ HOURS PER WEEK

NOT SPECIFIED

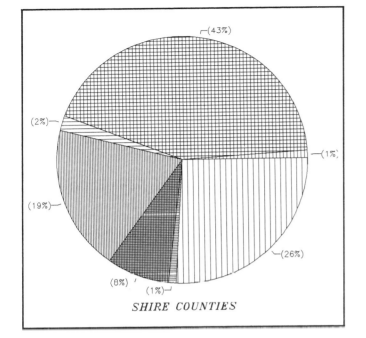

(43%)

(2%)

(1%)

(19%)

(26%)

(8%)

(1%)

SHIRE COUNTIES

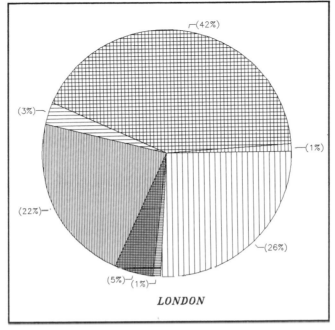

(42%)

(3%)

(1%)

(22%)

(26%)

(5%)

(1%)

LONDON

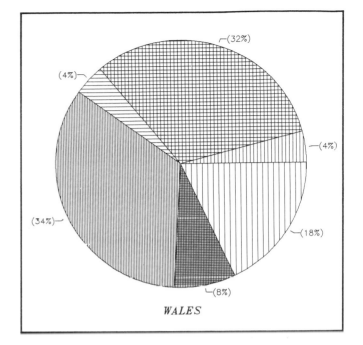

(32%)

(4%)

(4%)

(34%)

(18%)

(8%)

WALES

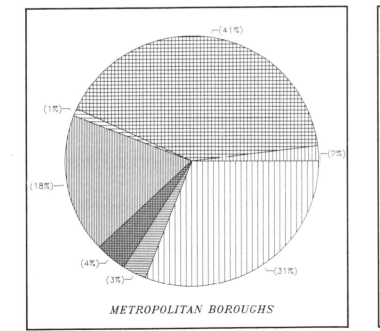

(41%)

(1%)

(2%)

(18%)

(31%)

(4%)

(3%)

METROPOLITAN BOROUGHS

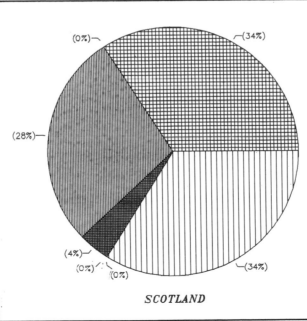

(0%)

(34%)

(28%)

(34%)

(4%)

(0%)

(0%)

SCOTLAND

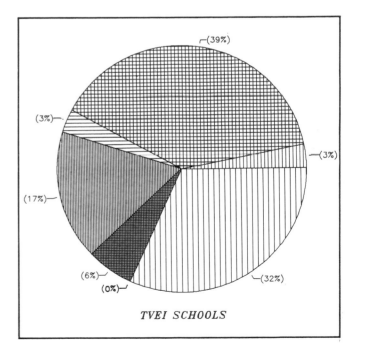

(39%)

(3%)

(3%)

(17%)

(32%)

(6%)

(0%)

TVEI SCHOOLS

5.1 (c)   Total amount of non-teaching time allocated specifically for careers

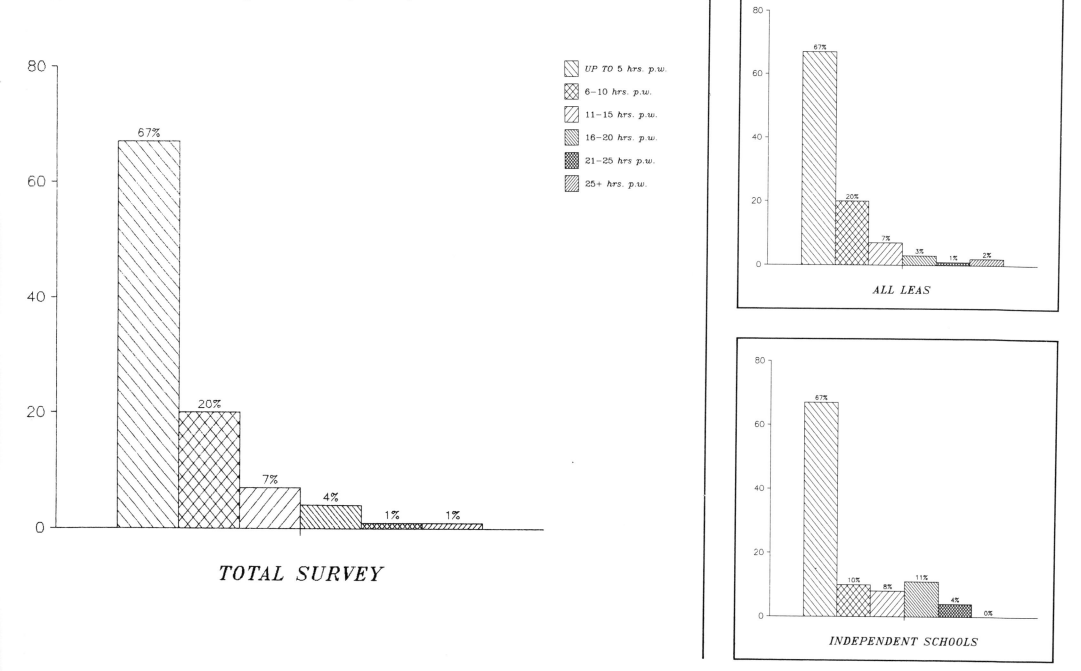

UP TO 5 hrs. p.w.

6–10 hrs. p.w.

11–15 hrs. p.w.

16–20 hrs. p.w.

21–25 hrs p.w.

25+ hrs. p.w.

TOTAL SURVEY

ALL LEAS

INDEPENDENT SCHOOLS

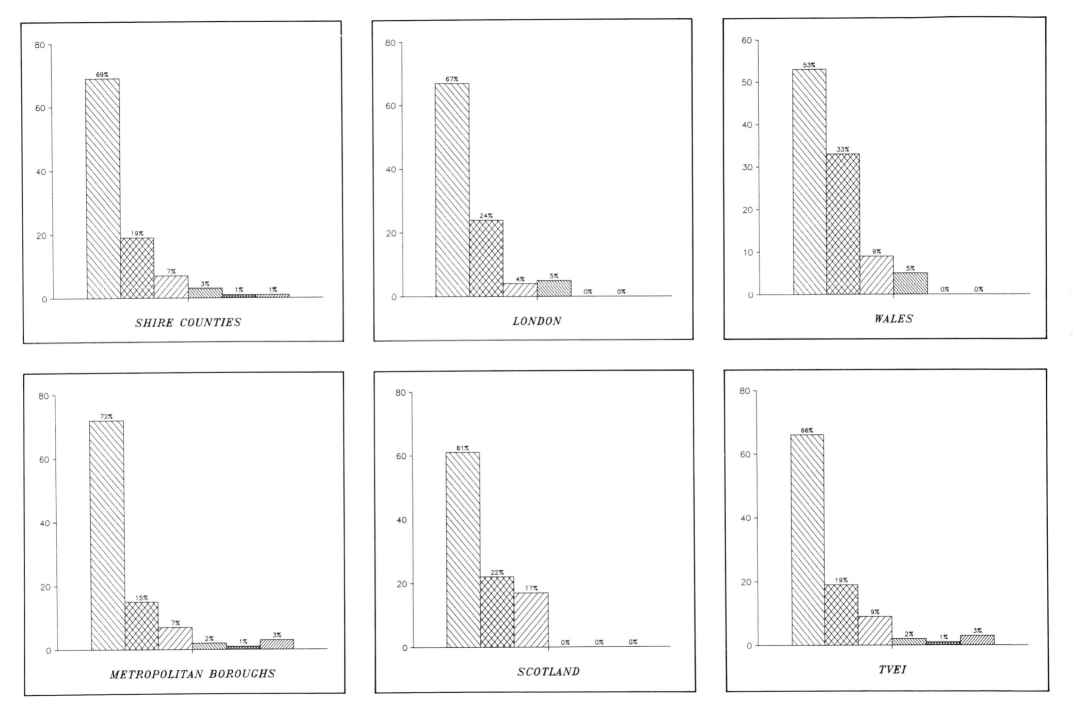

5.2 How does the head of careers spend his/her time? (Annual average)

ACTIVITY	0%	UP TO 10%	11-25%	25+%
1. TEACHING CAREERS	8%	34%	31%	26%
2. INTERVIEWING	7%	63%	20%	10%
3. ORGANISING INFORMATION	2%	83%	13%	2%
4. HELPING COLLEAGUES	13%	81%	6%	—
5. LIAISON WITH THE CAREERS SERVICE	5%	81%	13%	1%
6. VISITING	17%	76%	6%	1%
7. GENERAL ADMINISTRATION	1%	69%	26%	4%
8. PREPARING CAREERS MATERIALS	5%	80%	13%	2%
9. KEEPING UP TO DATE	6%	86%	8%	—
10. OTHER CAREERS ACTIVITIES	12%	75%	12%	1%
11. NON-CAREERS ACTIVITIES	5%	17%	17%	61%

TOTAL SURVEY

THE FIGURES ARE AGGRAGATED FROM SURVEY RESULTS

ACTIVITY	0%	UP TO 10%	11-25%	25+%
1	7%	33%	32%	28%
2	8%	66%	18%	8%
3	3%	84%	12%	1%
4	13%	81%	5%	1%
5	3%	82%	14%	1%
6	17%	76%	6%	1%
7	1%	69%	26%	4%
8	6%	81%	12%	1%
9	6%	86%	7%	1%
10	11%	76%	12%	1%
11	5%	16%	17%	62%

ALL LEAS

ACTIVITY	0%	UP TO 10%	11-25%	25+%
1	26%	50%	20%	4%
2	—	28%	43%	29%
3	—	53%	21%	6%
4	13%	81%	4%	2%
5	30%	66%	4%	—
6	15%	75%	6%	4%
7	—	63%	35%	2%
8	6%	70%	14%	—
9	4%	84%	12%	—
10	15%	58%	27%	—
11	5%	17%	4%	74%

INDEPENDENT SCHOOLS

SHIRE COUNTIES

ACTIVITY	0%	UP TO 10%	11-25%	25+%
1	10%	36%	34%	20%
2	8%	63%	20%	9%
3	3%	84%	13%	—
4	13%	80%	6%	1%
5	4%	82%	14%	—
6	17%	76%	6%	1%
7	2%	68%	27%	3%
8	5%	82%	11%	2%
9	7%	85%	8%	—
10	12%	77%	10%	1%
11	6%	13%	14%	67%

LONDON

ACTIVITY	0%	UP TO 10%	11-25%	25+%
1	6%	35%	30%	29%
2	5%	68%	18%	9%
3	—	85%	9%	6%
4	21%	75%	4%	—
5	—	89%	9%	2%
6	17%	83%	—	—
7	—	67%	26%	7%
8	5%	81%	10%	4%
9	3%	83%	8%	6%
10	11%	72%	15%	2%
11	1%	22%	16%	61%

WALES

ACTIVITY	0%	UP TO 10%	11-25%	25+%
1	4%	26%	37%	33%
2	5%	67%	20%	8%
3	2%	86%	12%	—
4	11%	83%	6%	—
5	2%	85%	11%	2%
6	15%	73%	12%	—
7	2%	64%	34%	—
8	6%	76%	17%	1%
9	7%	84%	9%	—
10	10%	77%	13%	—
11	2%	20%	28%	50%

METROPOLITAN BOROUGHS

ACTIVITY	0%	UP TO 10%	11-25%	25+%
1	3%	24%	36%	37%
2	10%	73%	13%	4%
3	4%	79%	15%	2%
4	10%	84%	6%	—
5	4%	79%	15%	2%
6	13%	77%	9%	1%
7	1%	70%	25%	4%
8	5%	80%	14%	1%
9	4%	85%	11%	—
10	11%	77%	12%	—
11	4%	21%	24%	51%

SCOTLAND

ACTIVITY	0%	UP TO 10%	11-25%	25+%
1	18%	50%	23%	7%
2	7%	60%	25%	8%
3	—	92%	0%	—
4	17%	79%	4%	—
5	—	89%	11%	—
6	32%	68%	—	—
7	—	69%	28%	3%
8	15%	65%	20%	—
9	8%	84%	4%	4%
10	7%	86%	7%	—
11		20%	20%	60%

TVEI SCHOOLS

ACTIVITY	0%	UP TO 10%	11-25%	25+%
1	7%	30%	39%	24%
2	7%	62%	22%	4%
3	2%	87%	10%	1%
4	12%	82%	6%	—
5	1%	83%	14%	2%
6	14%	80%	6%	—
7	3%	69%	26%	2%
8	5%	78%	16%	1%
9	4%	87%	9%	—
10	15%	71%	12%	2%
11	4%	18%	26%	52%

5.3 Average number of hours the head of careers gives of their own time to the careers department each week

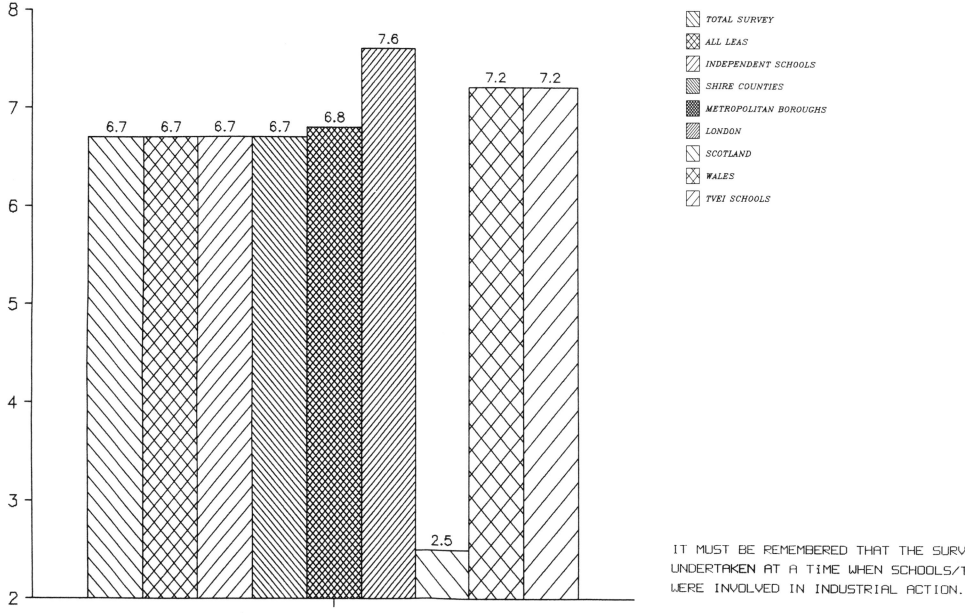

Legend:
- TOTAL SURVEY
- ALL LEAS
- INDEPENDENT SCHOOLS
- SHIRE COUNTIES
- METROPOLITAN BOROUGHS
- LONDON
- SCOTLAND
- WALES
- TVEI SCHOOLS

IT MUST BE REMEMBERED THAT THE SURVEY WAS UNDERTAKEN AT A TIME WHEN SCHOOLS/TEACHERS WERE INVOLVED IN INDUSTRIAL ACTION.

	TOTAL SURVEY	ALL LEAS	INDEP. SCHOOLS	SHIRE COUNTIES	MET BOROUGHS	LONDON	SCOTLAND	WALES	TVEI SCHOOLS
5.4 CLERICAL HELP AVAILABLE TO CAREERS DEPARTMENTS	74%	75%	72%	74%	80%	60%	82%	81%	74%
IS A SPECIFIC AMOUNT ALLOCATED TO CAREERS DEPARTMENTS	7%	7%	8%	7%	4%	13%	4%	4%	11%
WHERE YES HOW MUCH EACH WEEK ? UP TO 5 HRS	78%	79%	72%	79%	88%	73%	75%	100%	68%
6-10 HRS	9%	9%	10%	10%	4%	18%	—	—	14%
11-15 HRS	2%	2%	—	3%	4%	—	—	—	7%
16-20 HRS	5%	4%	6%	3%	4%	—	25%	—	7%
21-25 HRS	3%	3%	6%	4%	—	—	—	—	4%
25+ HRS	3%	3%	6%	1%	—	9%	—	—	—

	TOTAL SURVEY	ALL LEAS	INDEP SCHOOLS	SHIRE COUNTIES	MET BOROUGHS	LONDON	SCOTLAND	WALES	TVEI SCHOOLS
5.5 % OF CAREERS DEPARTMENTS HAVING OWN STUDENT RECORDS	67%	66%	73%	68%	62%	72%	42%	61%	63%
% WHICH GIVE CAREERS SERVICE OPEN ACCESS	81%	85%	42%	84%	88%	85%	60%	89%	83%
% OF SCHOOLS WITH STUDENT RECORD SYSTEM	96%	96%	93%	97%	96%	89%	100%	97%	100%
% OF CAREERS DEPARTMENTS WITH ACCESS TO THIS	93%	94%	88%	95%	89%	95%	91%	100%	95%
% OF CAREERS SERVICES WITH ACCESS TO SCHOOL RECORDS	44%	46%	17%	45%	44%	37%	30%	55%	48%
5.6 % OF SCHOOLS WITH A "PUPIL PROFILE" SYSTEM	33%	33%	28%	35%	29%	19%	71%	32%	54%
CAREERS DEPARTMENT'S INVOLVEMENT IN THIS — MINOR WAY	27%	28%	18%	24%	38%	12%	30%	27%	36%
SAME AS THE OTHER DEPTS	39%	39%	45%	40%	30%	76%	25%	27%	39%
MAJOR WAY	34%	33%	37%	36%	32%	12%	45%	46%	25%
5.7 % OF SCHOOLS WITH 3RD YEAR "OPTIONS" SYSTEM	94%	94%	84%	94%	96%	94%	100%	100%	96%
CAREERS DEPARTMENT'S INVOLVEMENT IN "OPTIONS" — MAJOR	65%	65%	58%	67%	64%	63%	73%	61%	64%
SAME AS THE OTHER DEPTS	12%	12%	18%	13%	6%	13%	3%	19%	10%
MINOR	19%	19%	21%	16%	25%	21%	21%	17%	22%
NO PART	4%	4%	3%	4%	5%	3%	3%	3%	4%
5.8 % OF CAREERS DEPTS PRODUCING INFORMATION ON OCCUPATIONAL SIGNIFICANCE OF SUBJECTS	51%	51%	54%	51%	49%	40%	62%	60%	54%

		TOTAL SURVEY	ALL LEAS	INDEP SCHOOLS	SHIRE COUNTIES	METRO BOROUGHS	LONDON	SCOTLAND	WALES	TVEI SCHOOLS
% OF LOCAL CAREERS ASSOCIATIONS		74%	74%	77%	77%	73%	81%	31%	56%	68%
ATTENDANCE	REGULAR	42%	44%	18%	47%	38%	47%	9%	31%	40%
	FREQUENT	22%	22%	22%	21%	24%	32%	9%	20%	22%
	RARE	24%	23%	44%	23%	22%	13%	27%	23%	25%
	NOT AT ALL	12%	11%	16%	9%	16%	8%	55%	26%	13%
ACTIVITIES IN WHICH THE ASSOCIATION ENGAGES (% OF ASSOCIATIONS)	TRAINING	26%	27%	18%	28%	29%	42%	3%	26%	26%
	COORDINATION OF WORK EXP	13%	13%	12%	13%	18%	12%	3%	11%	16%
	WRITING CURRICULUM MATERIALS	5%	5%	—	4%	7%	7%	—	11%	7%
	LIAISON WITH CAREERS SERV	52%	53%	30%	57%	49%	58%	17%	44%	49%
	TOPICAL DISCUSSIONS	57%	60%	42%	64%	58%	67%	21%	35%	59%
	SHARING RESOURCES	22%	22%	19%	22%	25%	27%	3%	16%	26%
	EVALUATING MATERIALS	22%	23%	11%	23%	21%	31%	3%	16%	24%
	WRITE AND AGREE POLICY STATEMENTS	11%	12%	5%	9%	14%	25%	—	14%	17%
	VISITS TO INDUSTRY ETC	42%	43%	33%	49%	39%	42%	3%	23%	37%

6.2 (a) NUMBER OF CAREERS OFFICERS WORKING WITH THE SCHOOL ON A REGULAR BASIS

	TOTAL SURVEY	ALL LEAS	INDEP SCHOOLS	SHIRE COUNTIES	MET BOROUGHS	LONDON	SCOTLAND	WALES	TVEI SCHOOLS
NONE	5%	2%	46%	2%	1%	3%	—	—	1%
ONE	54%	55%	44%	56%	57%	53%	61%	28%	49%
TWO	33%	35%	10%	36%	28%	36%	28%	65%	43%
THREE	7%	7%	—	5%	13%	8%	11%	7%	5%
FOUR	1%	1%	—	1%	1%	—	—	—	2%
FIVE	*	*	—	*	—	—	—	—	—

* ONE SCHOOL.

6.2 (b) AVERAGE WEEKLY TOTAL AMOUNT OF CAREERS OFFICER TIME ALLOCATED TO THE SCHOOL

	TOTAL SURVEY	ALL LEAS	INDEP SCHOOLS	SHIRE COUNTIES	MET BOROUGHS	LONDON	SCOTLAND	WALES	TVEI SCHOOLS
UP TO 5 HOURS PER WEEK	57%	56%	96%	60%	50%	63%	53%	40%	57%
6-10 HOURS PER WEEK	32%	33%	4%	32%	35%	30%	32%	37%	31%
11-15 HOURS PER WEEK	8%	8%	—	6%	11%	7%	15%	18%	8%
16-20 HOURS PER WEEK	2%	2%	—	2%	1%	—	—	5%	3%
21-25 HOURS PER WEEK	—	1%	—	—	2%	—	—	—	—
MORE THAN 25 HOURS PER WEEK	1%	1%	—	*	1%	—	—	—	1%

* 2 SCHOOLS

6.2 (c) HOW IS A CAREERS OFFICER'S 'SCHOOL TIME' DIVIDED UP ?

ACTIVITY	0%	UP TO 10%	11-50%	50+%
1. INTERVIEWING INDIVIDUAL STUDENTS	1%	2%	13%	84%
2. INTERVIEWING GROUPS OF STUDENTS	12%	56%	29%	3%
3. "TEACHING" CAREERS	59%	37%	3%	1%
4. TALKING TO PARENTS	19%	74%	4%	3%
5. ADVISING STAFF	41%	57%	2%	1%
6. ORGANISING WORK EXPERIENCE	84%	14%	1%	1%
7. VISITING STUDENTS ON WORK EXPERIENCE	90%	10%	—	—
8. ORGANISING CAREERS LIBRARY	81%	18%	—	1%
9. TRAINING STAFF	90%	9%	—	1%
10. HELPING WITH 3RD YEAR OPTIONS	38%	60%	2%	—
11. OTHER	52%	43%	5%	—

TOTAL SURVEY

THE FIGURES ARE AGGRAGATED FROM SURVEY RESULTS

ACTIVITY	0%	UP TO 10%	11-50%	50+%
1	1%	2%	13%	84%
2	11%	56%	29%	4%
3	59%	36%	4%	1%
4	19%	75%	5%	—
5	40%	58%	2%	
6	83%	16%	1%	—
7	89%	10%	1%	
8	81%	19%	1%	—
9	90%	9%	1%	—
10	37%	60%	3%	—
11	51%	44%	5%	—

ALL LEAS

ACTIVITY	0%	UP TO 10%	11-50%	50+%
1	4%	6%	10%	80%
2	28%	47%	20%	5%
3	64%	36%	—	—
4	32%	48%	20%	—
5	59%	35%	—	6%
6	92%	—	8%	—
7	100%	—	—	—
8	93%	7%	—	—
9	100%	—	—	—
10	61%	28%	6%	5%
11	79%	7%	14%	—

INDEPENDENT SCHOOLS

SHIRE COUNTIES

ACTIVITY	0%	UP TO 10%	11-50%	50+%
1	1%	2%	15%	82%
2	11%	52%	31%	6%
3	63%	34%	3%	—
4	16%	77%	5%	2%
5	44%	55%	1%	—
6	85%	14%	1%	—
7	91%	9%	—	—
8	82%	18%	—	—
9	92%	8%	—	—
10	42%	57%	1%	—
11	56%	40%	4%	—

SHIRE COUNTIES

LONDON

ACTIVITY	0%	UP TO 10%	11-50%	50+%
1	3%	6%	10%	81%
2	13%	38%	38%	11%
3	51%	46%	—	3%
4	23%	65%	10%	2%
5	36%	61%	3%	—
6	90%	10%	—	—
7	100%	—	—	—
8	94%	3%	—	3%
9	87%	10%	—	5%
10	33%	57%	8%	2%
11	39%	61%	—	—

LONDON

WALES

ACTIVITY	0%	UP TO 10%	11-50%	50+%
1	—	—	2%	98%
2	7%	77%	16%	—
3	68%	32%	—	—
4	26%	69%	5%	—
5	30%	70%	—	—
6	81%	19%	—	—
7	93%	7%	—	—
8	83%	17%	—	—
9	100%	—	—	—
10	20%	80%	—	—
11	54%	46%	—	—

WALES

METROPOLITAN BOROUGHS

ACTIVITY	0%	UP TO 10%	11-50%	50+%
1	—	—	11%	89%
2	11%	62%	25%	2%
3	58%	35%	7%	—
4	23%	73%	4%	—
5	43%	55%	2%	—
6	83%	14%	3%	—
7	89%	10%	1%	—
8	86%	13%	1%	—
9	91%	9%	—	—
10	38%	58%	4%	—
11	45%	49%	6%	—

METROPOLITAN BOROUGHS

SCOTLAND

ACTIVITY	0%	UP TO 10%	11-50%	50+%
1	—	—	5%	95%
2	—	59%	33%	8%
3	39%	43%	18%	—
4	30%	70%	—	—
5	14%	86%	—	—
6	81%	19%	—	—
7	88%	6%	—	6%
8	43%	52%	—	5%
9	76%	18%	—	4%
10	29%	71%	—	—
11	35%	65%	—	—

SCOTLAND

TVEI SCHOOLS

ACTIVITY	0%	UP TO 10%	11-50%	50+%
1	2%	1%	14%	84%
2	10%	56%	32%	2%
3	57%	41%	2%	—
4	24%	72%	3%	1%
5	39%	59%	2%	—
6	73%	23%	4%	—
7	80%	14%	3%	3%
8	74%	22%	4%	2%
9	82%	16%	—	2%
10	34%	64%	2%	—
11	45%	48%	7%	—

TVEI SCHOOLS

6.2 (d)   Do other members of the careers service visit the school?

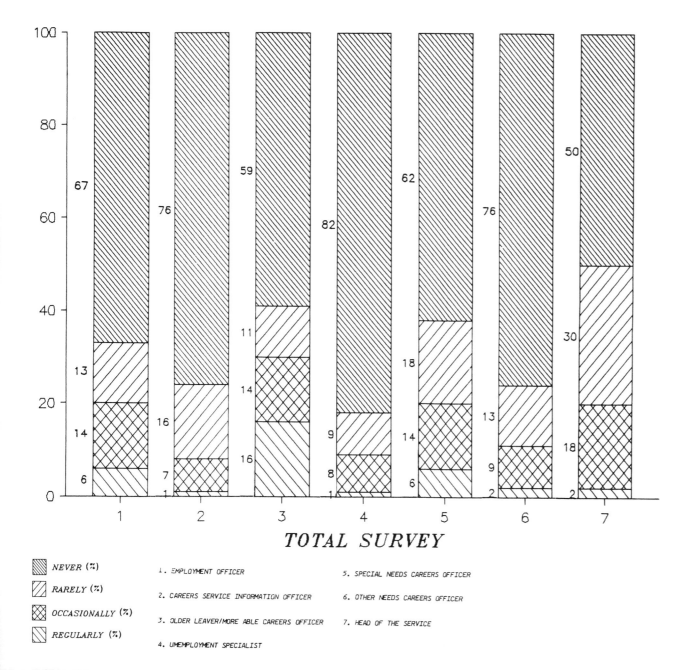

TOTAL SURVEY

NEVER (%)

RARELY (%)

OCCASIONALLY (%)

REGULARLY (%)

1. EMPLOYMENT OFFICER
2. CAREERS SERVICE INFORMATION OFFICER
3. OLDER LEAVER/MORE ABLE CAREERS OFFICER
4. UMEMPLOYMENT SPECIALIST
5. SPECIAL NEEDS CAREERS OFFICER
6. OTHER NEEDS CAREERS OFFICER
7. HEAD OF THE SERVICE

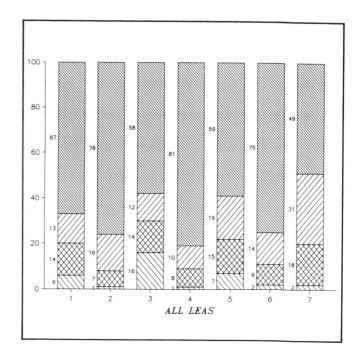

ALL LEAS

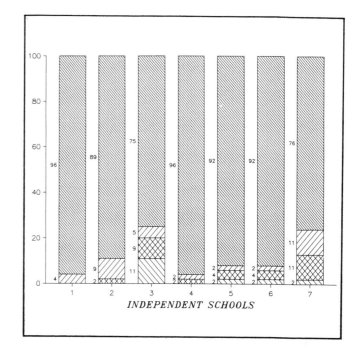

INDEPENDENT SCHOOLS

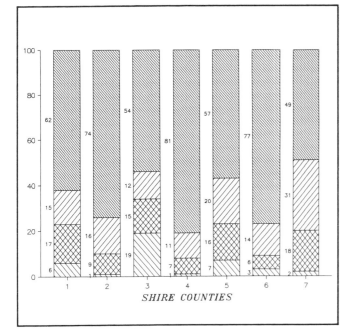

SHIRE COUNTIES

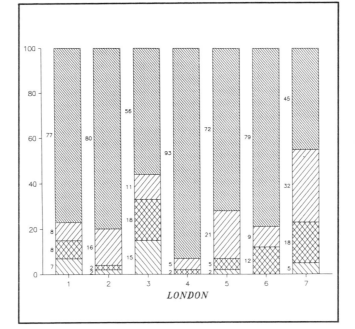

LONDON

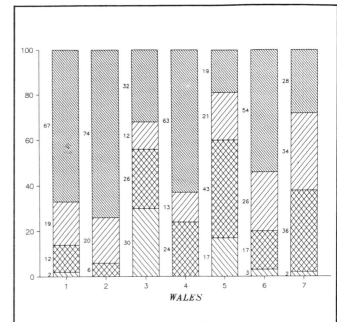

WALES

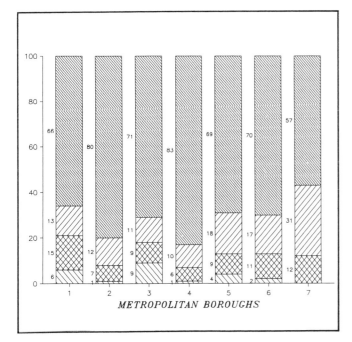

METROPOLITAN BOROUGHS

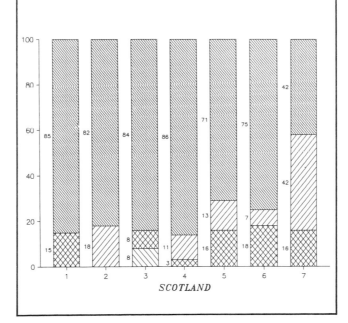

SCOTLAND

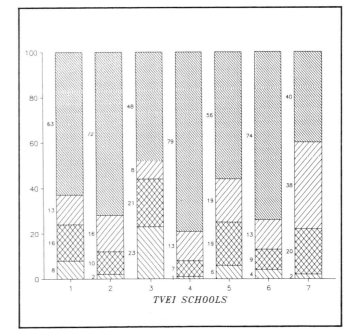

TVEI SCHOOLS

6.2 (e) Where is the nearest careers office?

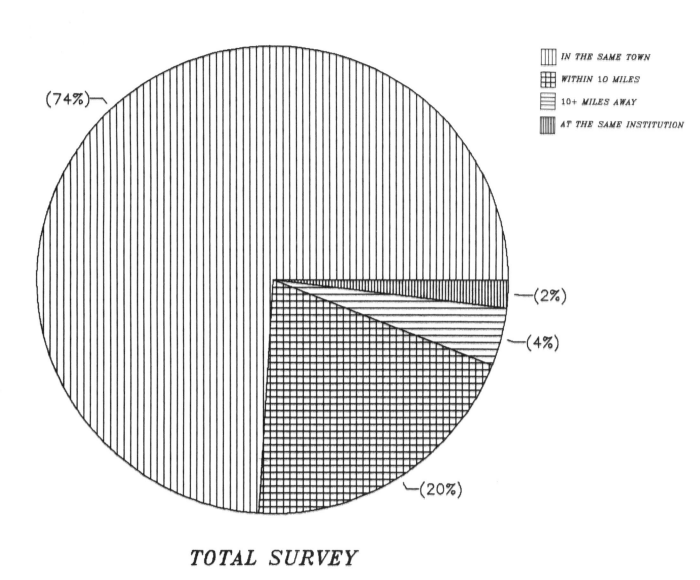

IN THE SAME TOWN
WITHIN 10 MILES
10+ MILES AWAY
AT THE SAME INSTITUTION

(74%)
—(2%)
—(4%)
—(20%)

TOTAL SURVEY

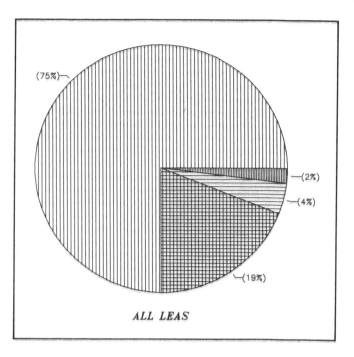

(75%)
—(2%)
—(4%)
—(19%)

ALL LEAS

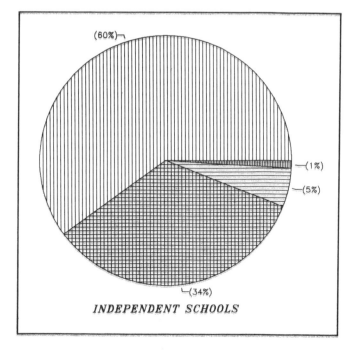

(60%)
—(1%)
—(5%)
—(34%)

INDEPENDENT SCHOOLS

PAGE 66

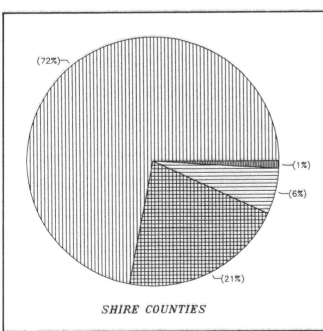

(72%)

(1%)

(6%)

(21%)

SHIRE COUNTIES

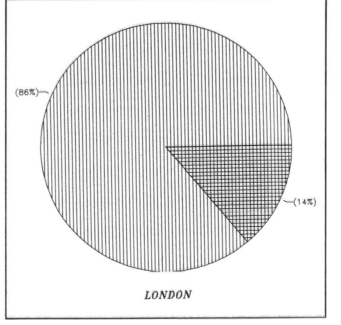

(86%)

(14%)

LONDON

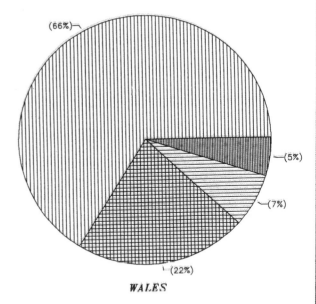

(66%)

(5%)

(7%)

(22%)

WALES

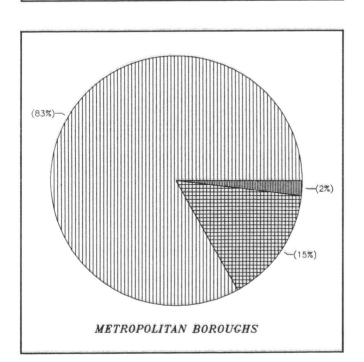

(83%)

(2%)

(15%)

METROPOLITAN BOROUGHS

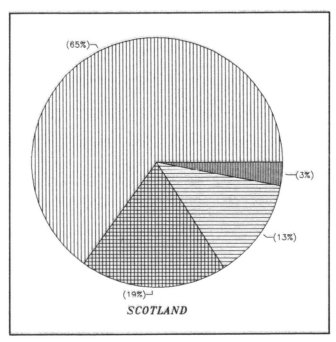

(65%)

(3%)

(13%)

(19%)

SCOTLAND

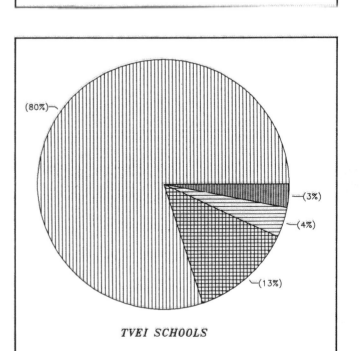

(80%)

(3%)

(4%)

(13%)

TVEI SCHOOLS

6.2 (f) Does the careers service

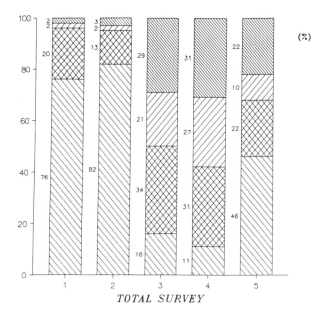

TOTAL SURVEY

Legend:
- NEVER (%)
- RARELY
- OCCASIONALLY (%)
- REGULARLY (%)

(%)

1. PROVIDE LOCAL CAREERS INFORMATION ?

2. PROVIDE DETAILS OF EMPLOYMENT/ TRAINING FOR YOUNG PEOPLE ?

3. ARRANGE TRAINING COURSES FOR TEACHERS ?

4. INVITE TEACHERS TO JOIN IN VISITS TO EMPLOYERS ?

5. ORGANISE OR OFFER ADMIN SUPPORT FOR LOCAL CAREERS ASSOC ?

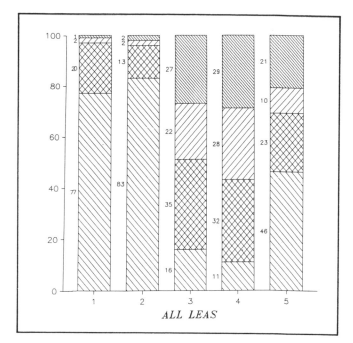

ALL LEAS

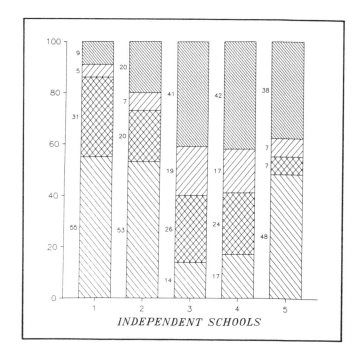

INDEPENDENT SCHOOLS

6.2 (g)

TOTAL SURVEY   (i) % OF CAREERS SERVICES PROVIDING A CAREERS
EDUCATION RESOURCE CENTRE 84%
(ii) WHO ALLOW MATERIALS TO BE BORROWED 90%

ALL LEAS	(i) 83%	INDEPENDENT SCHOOLS	(i) 90%
	(ii) 92%		(ii) 70%
SHIRE COUNTIES	(i) 85%	METROPOLITAN BOROUGHS	(i) 91%
	(ii) 90%		(ii) 97%
LONDON	(i) 76%	SCOTLAND	(i) 89%
	(ii) 86%		(ii) 91%
WALES	(i) 55%	TVEI SCHOOLS	(i) 78%
	(ii) 90%		(ii) 88%

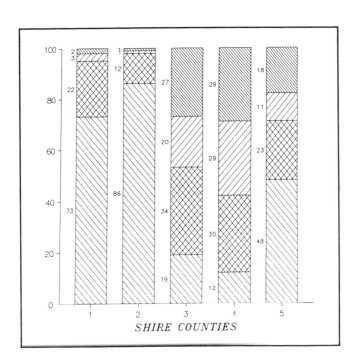

SHIRE COUNTIES

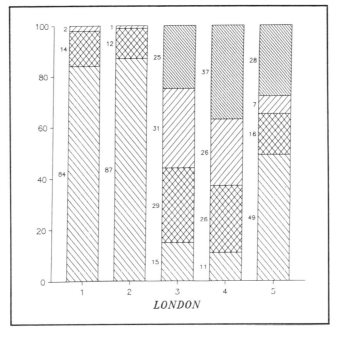

LONDON

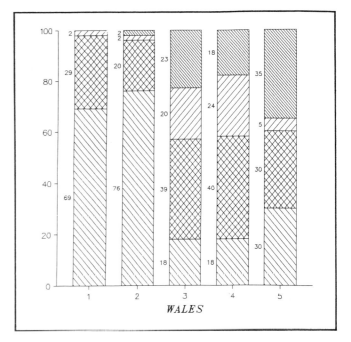

WALES

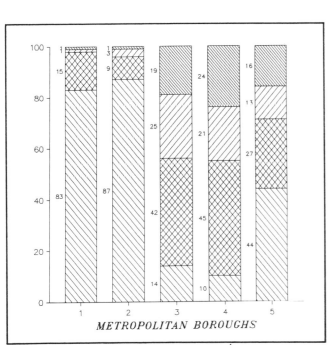

METROPOLITAN BOROUGHS

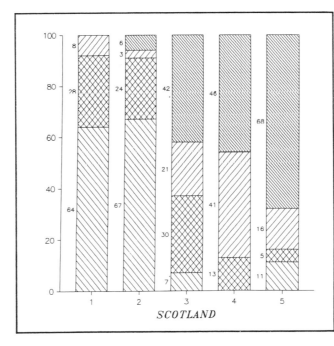

SCOTLAND

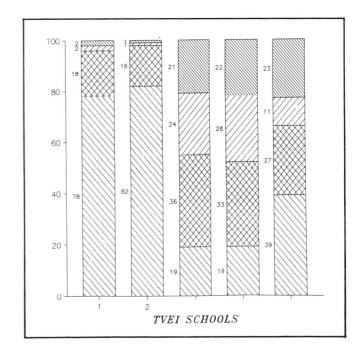

TVEI SCHOOLS

6.3 Employers

(a) % of schools having regular contact with a wide range of
employers and/or employer organisations and/or training
organisations 80%

(b) Contact is mainly with
the careers dept 82% other depts 4% roughly equal 14%

(c) Frequency of employers participating in the schools careers work
Frequently 12% Fairly regularly 37% Rarely 43% Never 8%

(d) % of schools organising work experience   87%
% of schools having work experience organised from outside
the school 37%

(e) Policy for work experience : Open and available to all students 64%
Open only to particular groups of students 36%.

(f) (i) Annual average number of students participating in work
experience 87.

(ii) Annual average number of employers used for work experience 49.

(h) Frequency of careers conventions
Never 41% Occasionally 19%   Every 2 years 22%   Every year 18%.

(i) Average number of employers participating in careers conventions 42.

TOTAL SURVEY

(a)	81%	—	—	—
(b)	81%	4%	15%	—
(c)	12%	37%	44%	7%
(d)	88%	37%	—	—
(e)	65%	35%	—	—
(f)	90	51	—	—
(h)	41%	20%	22%	17%
(i)	42	—	—	—

ALL LEAS

(a)	66%	—	—	—
(b)	93%	2%	5%	—
(c)	12%	45%	38%	5%
(d)	79%	44%	—	—
(e)	55%	45%	—	—
(f)	40	25	—	—
(h)	38%	16%	25%	25%
(i)	49	—	—	—

INDEPENDENT SCHOOLS

SHIRE COUNTIES

(a)	84%	—	—	—
(b)	82%	4%	14%	—
(c)	15%	37%	42%	6%
(d)	89%	54%	—	—
(e)	73%	27%	—	—
(f)	101	58	—	—
(h)	42%	16%	24%	18%
(i)	44	—	—	—

SHIRE COUNTIES

LONDON

(a)	81%	—	—	—
(b)	75%	6%	19%	—
(c)	8%	38%	46%	8%
(d)	92%	60%	—	—
(e)	54%	46%	—	—
(f)	66	45	—	—
(h)	39%	31%	16%	14%
(i)	42	—	—	—

LONDON

WALES

(a)	79%	—	—	—
(b)	82%	6%	12%	—
(c)	16%	40%	36%	8%
(d)	94%	31%	—	—
(e)	54%	46%	—	—
(f)	66	28	—	—
(h)	20%	20%	32%	28%
(i)	44	—	—	—

WALES

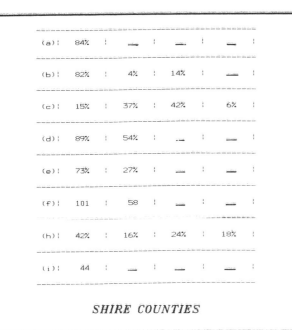

METROPOLITAN BOROUGHS

(a)	77%	—	—	—
(b)	84%	3%	13%	—
(c)	9%	36%	45%	10%
(d)	84%	42%	—	—
(e)	65%	35%	—	—
(f)	91	49	—	—
(h)	38%	28%	19%	14%
(i)	34	—	—	—

METROPOLITAN BOROUGHS

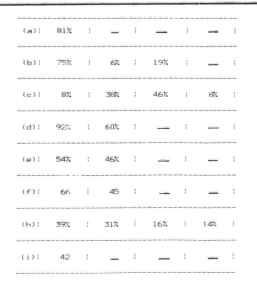

SCOTLAND

(a)	69%	—	—	—
(b)	71%	11%	18%	—
(c)	3%	43%	43%	11%
(d)	81%	32%	—	—
(e)	30%	70%	—	—
(f)	44	23	—	—
(h)	34%	26%	23%	17%
(i)	34	—	—	—

SCOTLAND

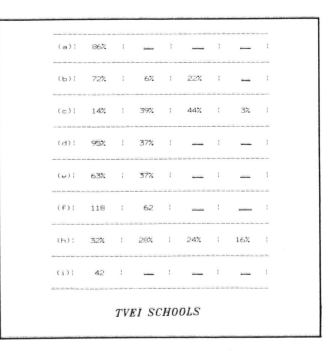

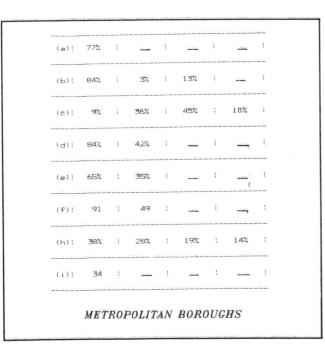

TVEI SCHOOLS

(a)	86%	—	—	—
(b)	72%	6%	22%	—
(c)	14%	39%	44%	3%
(d)	95%	37%	—	—
(e)	63%	37%	—	—
(f)	118	62	—	—
(h)	32%	28%	24%	16%
(i)	42	—	—	—

TVEI SCHOOLS

6.3 (g) Number of employers with which the careers department has contact each year (excluding work experience)

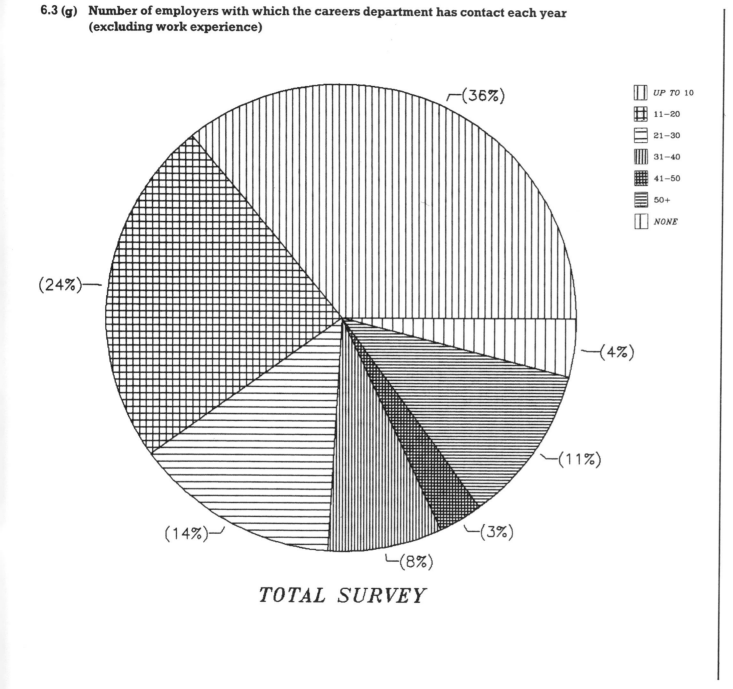

Legend:
- ||| UP TO 10
- ⊞ 11–20
- ☰ 21–30
- ||||| 31–40
- ▦ 41–50
- ☰ 50+
- || NONE

TOTAL SURVEY

(36%) (4%) (11%) (3%) (8%) (14%) (24%)

(36%) (3%) (11%) (3%) (8%) (14%) (25%)

ALL LEAS

(39%) (9%) (11%) (6%) (9%) (9%) (17%)

INDEPENDENT SCHOOLS

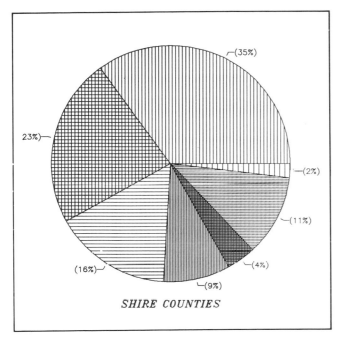

SHIRE COUNTIES

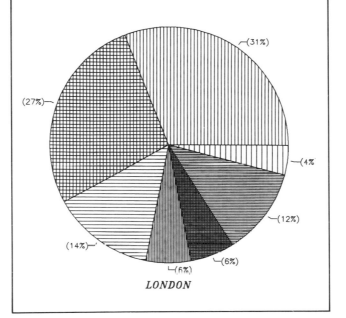

LONDON

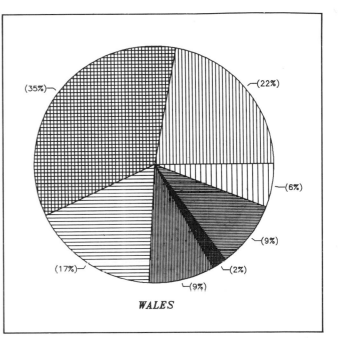

WALES

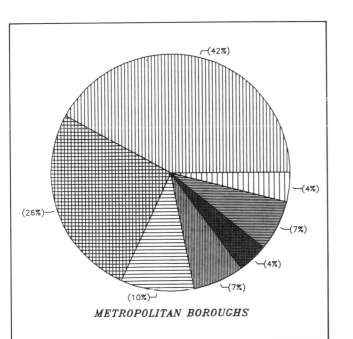

METROPOLITAN BOROUGHS

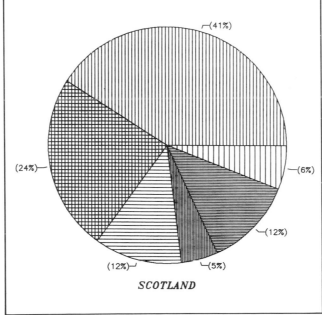

SCOTLAND

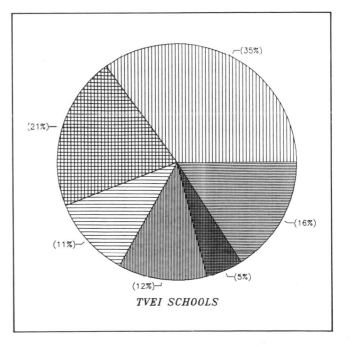

TVEI SCHOOLS

6.4 (b) Ways in which students are informed about further education courses

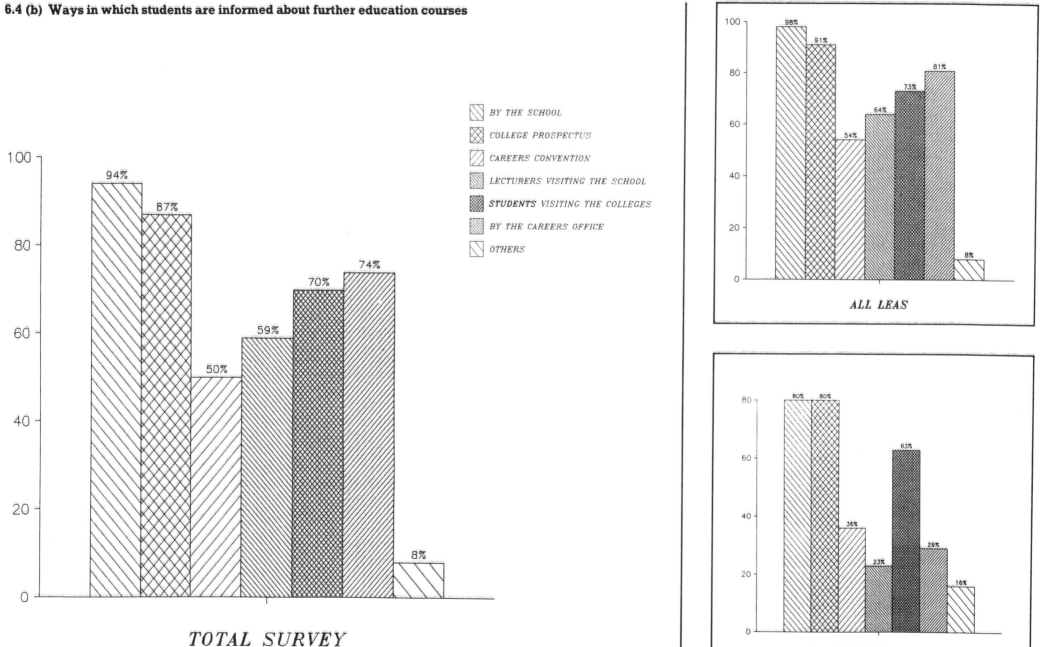

Legend:
- BY THE SCHOOL
- COLLEGE PROSPECTUS
- CAREERS CONVENTION
- LECTURERS VISITING THE SCHOOL
- *STUDENTS* VISITING THE COLLEGES
- BY THE CAREERS OFFICE
- OTHERS

TOTAL SURVEY

(Total Survey values: 94%, 87%, 50%, 59%, 70%, 74%, 8%)

ALL LEAS

(All LEAs values: 98%, 91%, 54%, 64%, 73%, 81%, 8%)

INDEPENDENT SCHOOLS

(Independent Schools values: 80%, 80%, 36%, 23%, 63%, 29%, 16%)

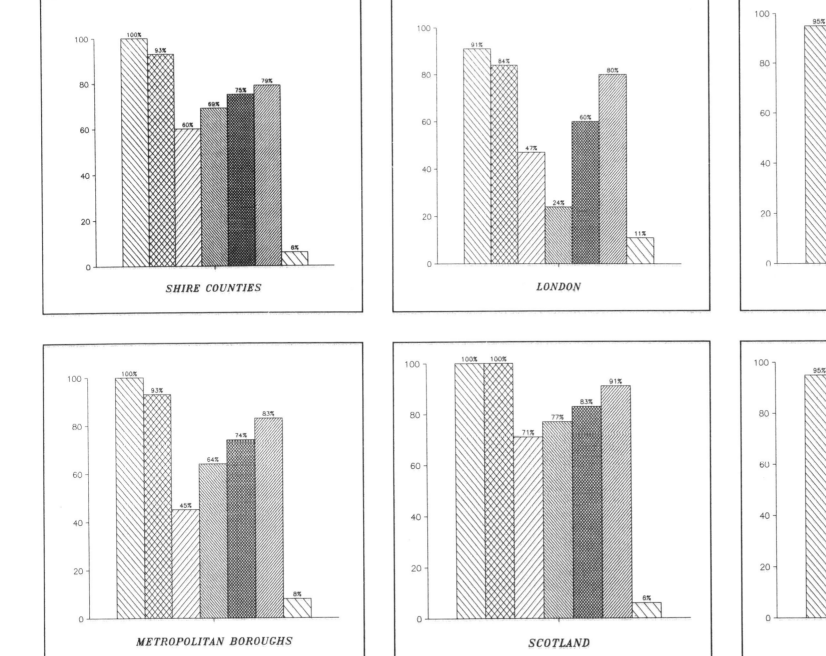

SHIRE COUNTIES

LONDON

WALES

METROPOLITAN BOROUGHS

SCOTLAND

TVEI SCHOOLS

6.4 (c)   Frequency of meetings between school staff and college staff

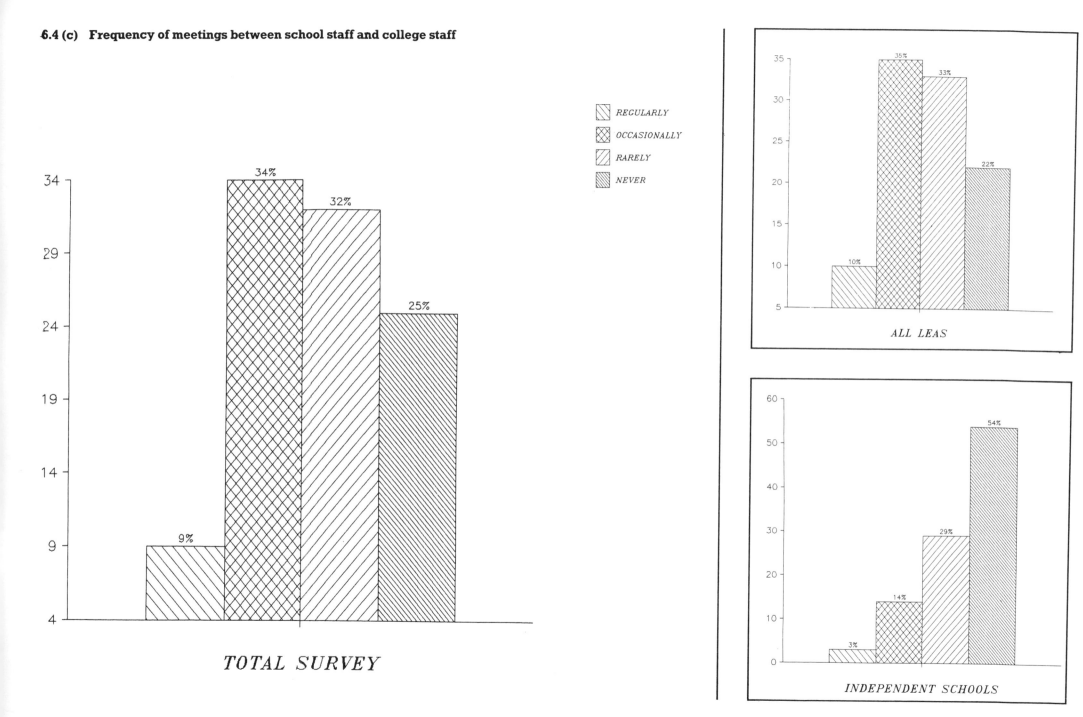

REGULARLY

OCCASIONALLY

RARELY

NEVER

TOTAL SURVEY

ALL LEAS

INDEPENDENT SCHOOLS

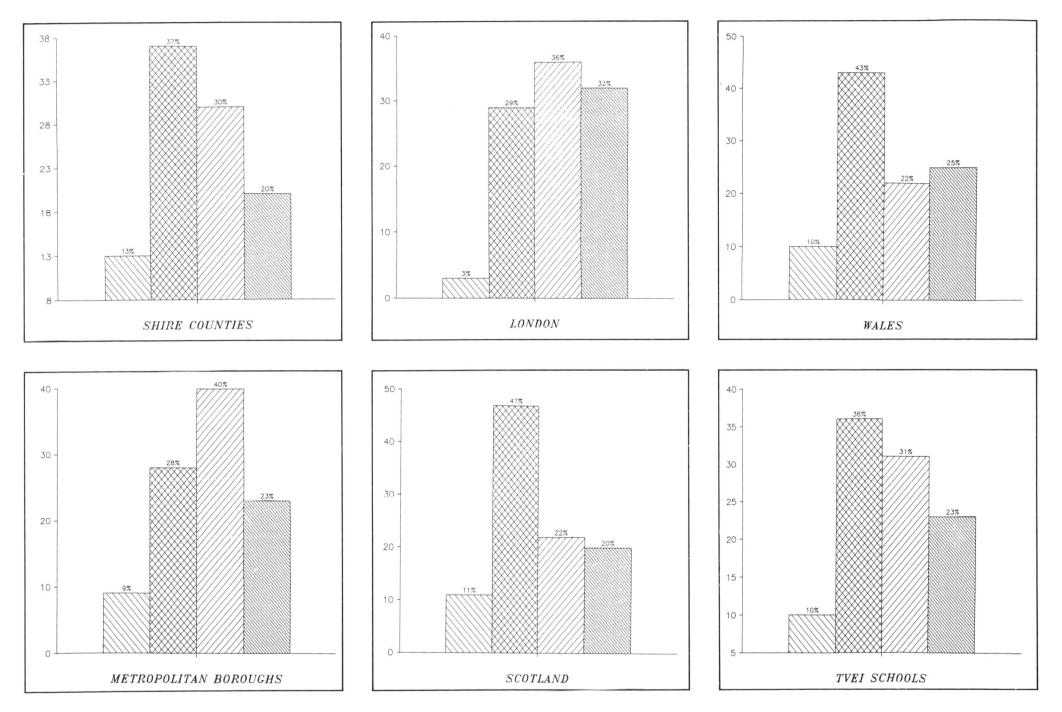

SHIRE COUNTIES

LONDON

WALES

METROPOLITAN BOROUGHS

SCOTLAND

TVEI SCHOOLS

6.5 (b) How students are informed about higher education

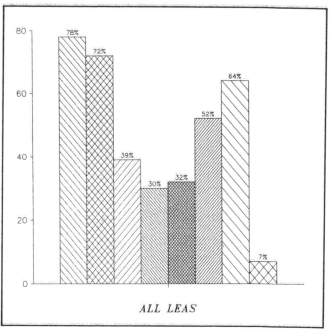

ALL LEAS

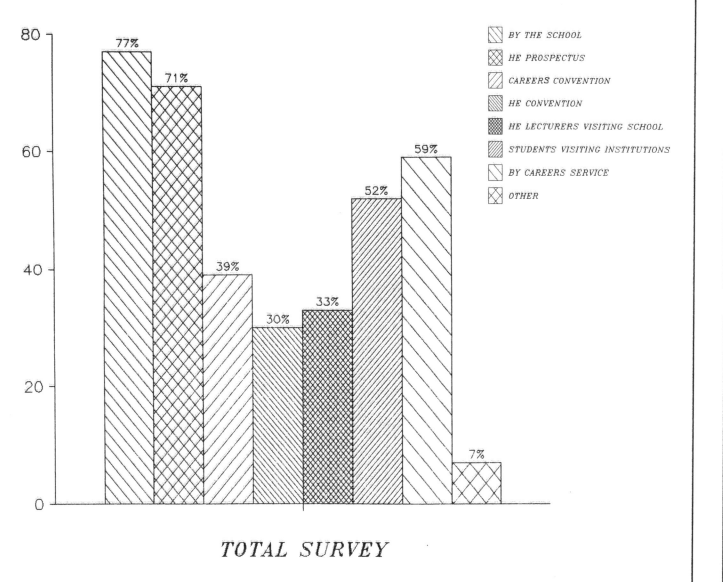

Legend:
- BY THE SCHOOL
- HE PROSPECTUS
- CAREERS CONVENTION
- HE CONVENTION
- HE LECTURERS VISITING SCHOOL
- STUDENTS VISITING INSTITUTIONS
- BY CAREERS SERVICE
- OTHER

TOTAL SURVEY

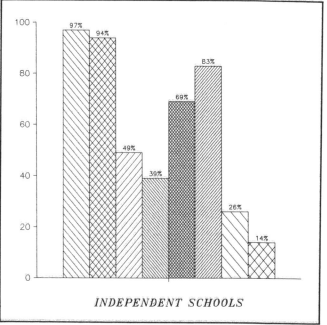

INDEPENDENT SCHOOLS

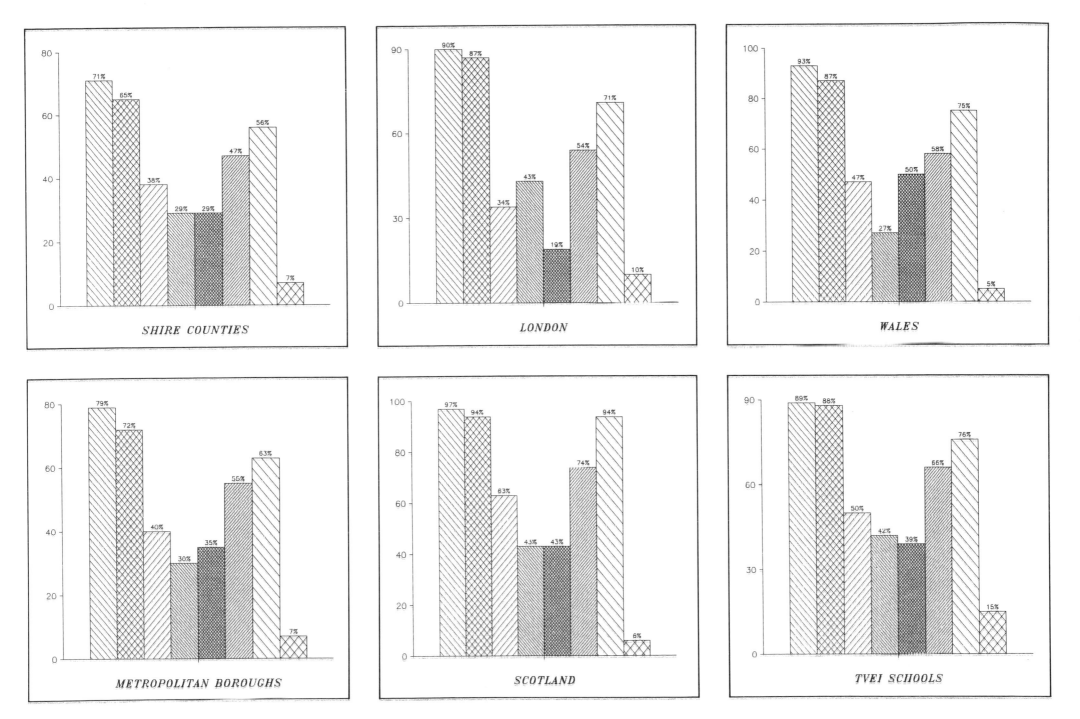

SHIRE COUNTIES

LONDON

WALES

METROPOLITAN BOROUGHS

SCOTLAND

TVEI SCHOOLS

6.6 (a) The main methods used by careers departments to communicate with parents

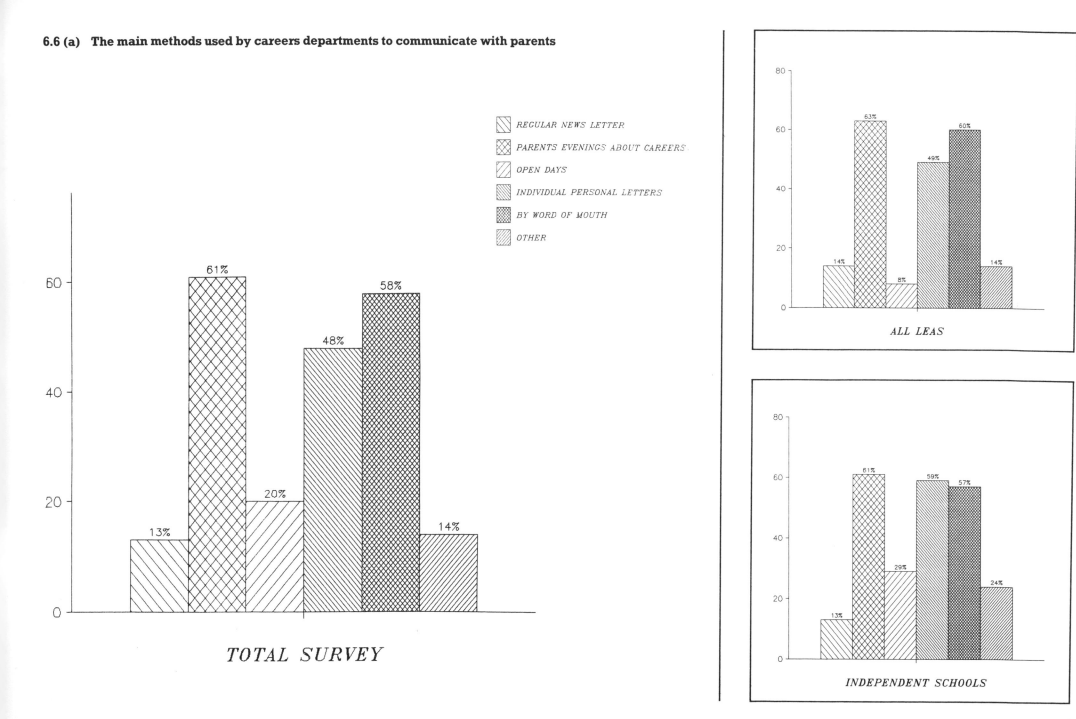

REGULAR NEWS LETTER

PARENTS EVENINGS ABOUT CAREERS.

OPEN DAYS

INDIVIDUAL PERSONAL LETTERS

BY WORD OF MOUTH

OTHER

TOTAL SURVEY

ALL LEAS

INDEPENDENT SCHOOLS

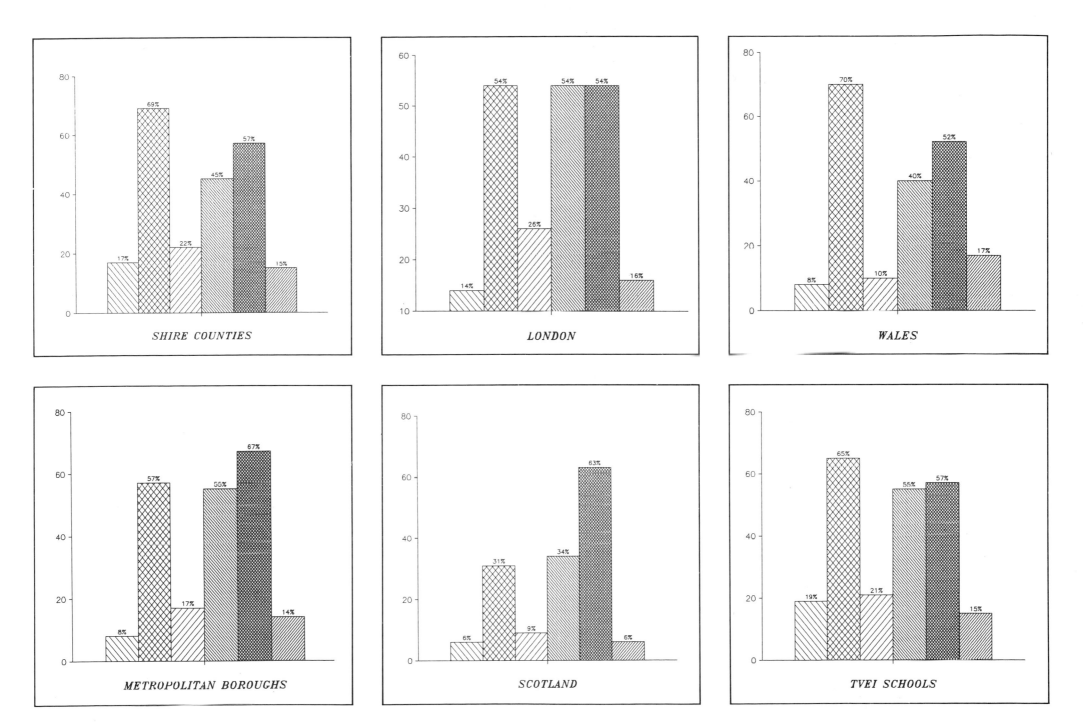

SHIRE COUNTIES

LONDON

WALES

METROPOLITAN BOROUGHS

SCOTLAND

TVEI SCHOOLS

6.6 (b)   The extent to which parents are used in the careers process

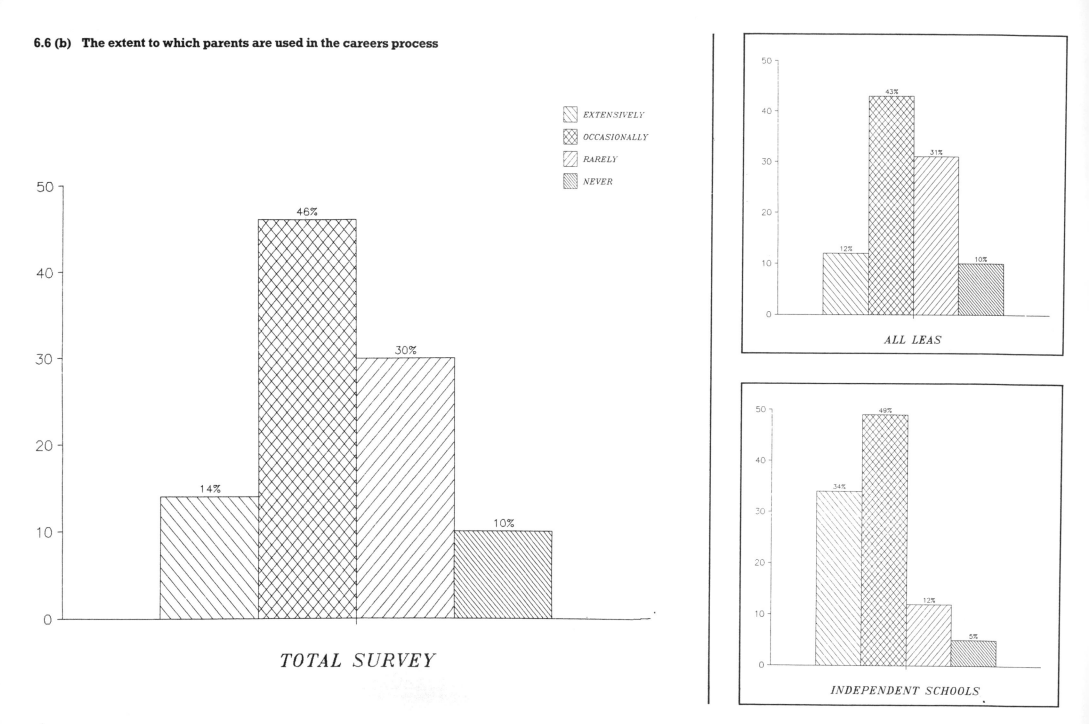

EXTENSIVELY

OCCASIONALLY

RARELY

NEVER

TOTAL SURVEY

46%

14%

30%

10%

ALL LEAS

43%

12%

31%

10%

INDEPENDENT SCHOOLS

49%

34%

12%

5%

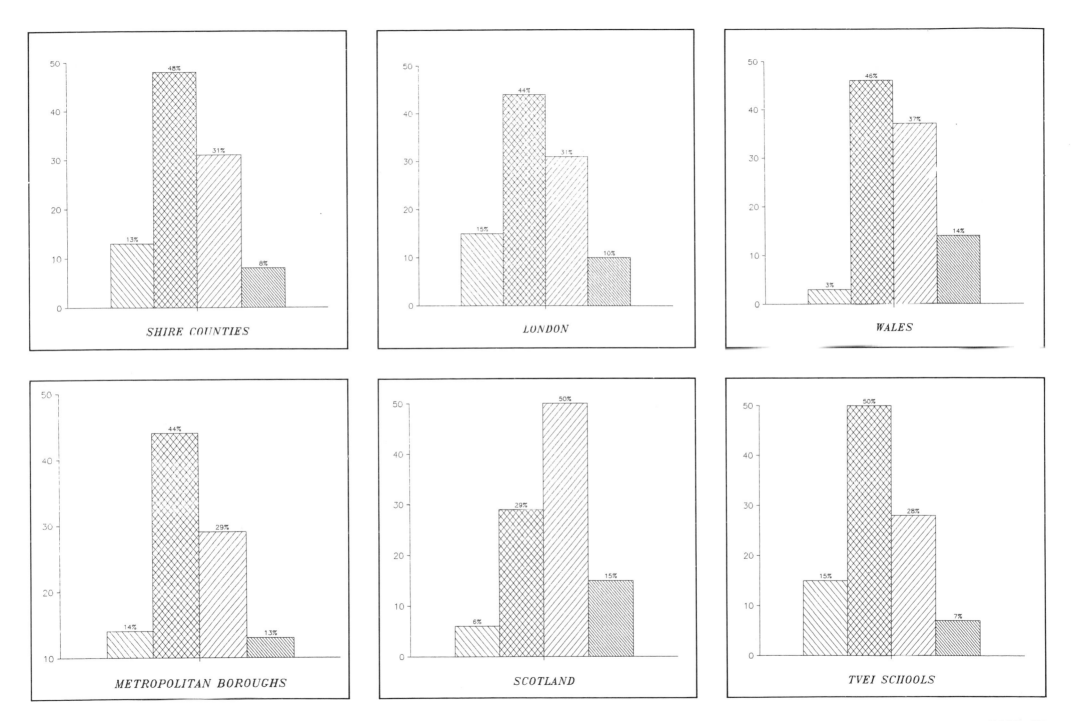

SHIRE COUNTIES

LONDON

WALES

METROPOLITAN BOROUGHS

SCOTLAND

TVEI SCHOOLS

6.7 (a)   % of schools attempting to use the experience of former students in the careers process

TOTAL SURVEY	67%	INDEPENDENT SCHOOLS	87%
ALL LEAS	65%	METROPOLITAN SCHOOLS	64%
SHIRE COUNTIES	69%	SCOTLAND	42%
LONDON	66%	TVEI SCHOOLS	65%
WALES	62%		

(b)   Extent to which this is done

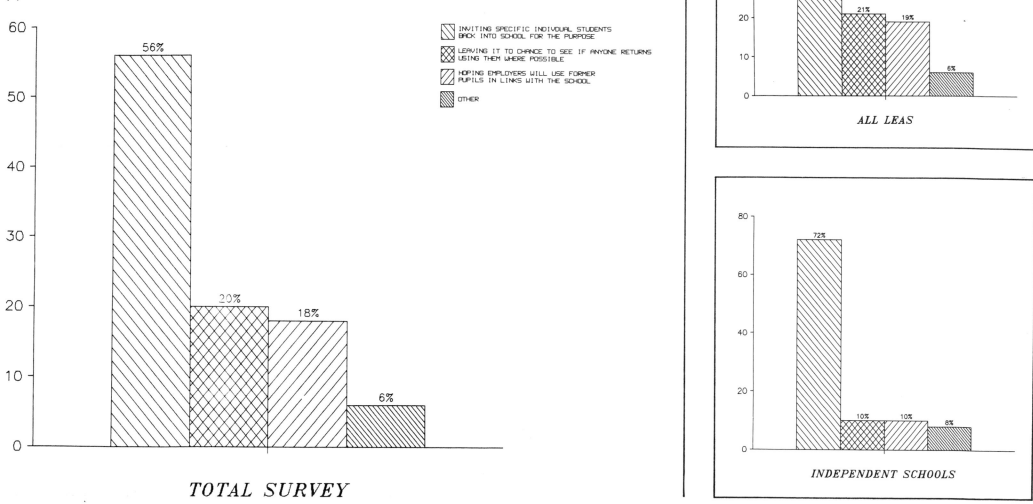

INVITING SPECIFIC INDIVIDUAL STUDENTS BACK INTO SCHOOL FOR THE PURPOSE

LEAVING IT TO CHANCE TO SEE IF ANYONE RETURNS USING THEM WHERE POSSIBLE

HOPING EMPLOYERS WILL USE FORMER PUPILS IN LINKS WITH THE SCHOOL

OTHER

TOTAL SURVEY

ALL LEAS

INDEPENDENT SCHOOLS

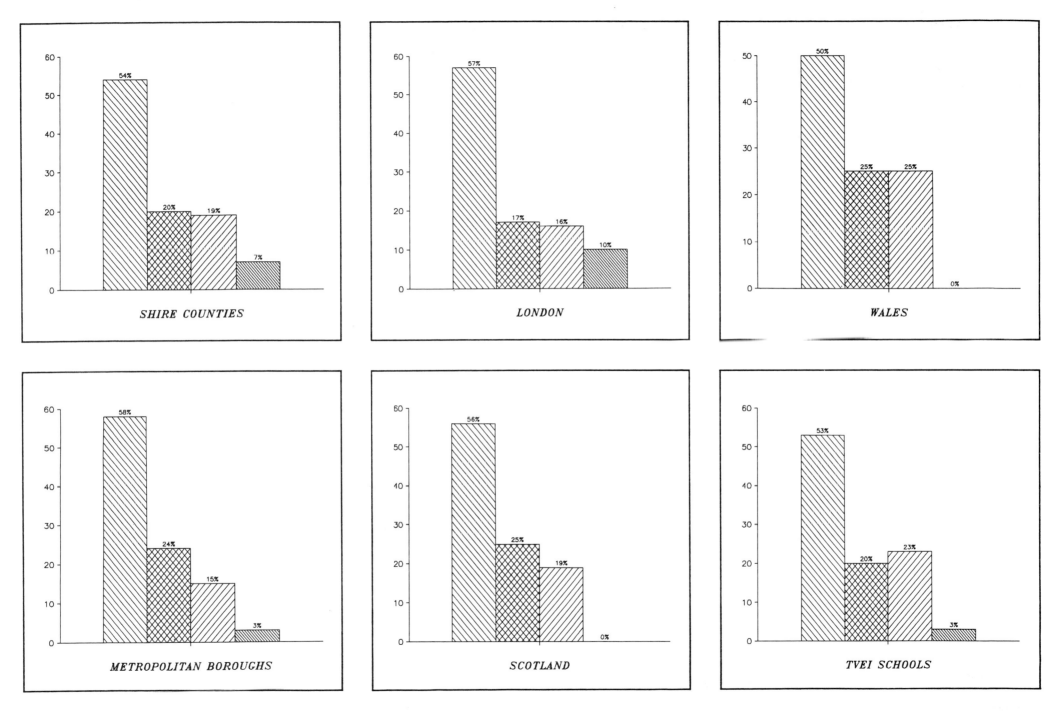

SHIRE COUNTIES

LONDON

WALES

METROPOLITAN BOROUGHS

SCOTLAND

TVEI SCHOOLS

This page has been intentionally left blank

V GENERAL IMPRESSIONS

The back page of the questionnaire gave respondents an opportunity to 'write any comments, observations etc that you want to make about the state of careers work in your school'. Just over half the returns had some written comments which elaborated upon the answers which had been given.

In general the more critical comments completely outweighed the complimentary comments which were included.

Clearly a number of teachers were well satisfied with what was going on in their schools, and it is important to recognise that the 'state of play' is not universally problematical. Comments such as 'flourishing' and 'thriving' were made, although it must be stated that these were rare. There does appear to be a number of schools, however, albeit small in percentage terms, who have taken careers work very seriously and provide the necessary manpower and resources to do the job properly.

A more significant number of the respondents commented in positive terms about the support which they received from their heads and/or the way in which form tutors were involved in a positive and committed way.

'With a whole school philosophy and commitment from the staff and the head for the importance of careers education and guidance there is much support for the work done in the careers centre.'

'The state of careers work in the school depends upon the attitude of the headteacher.'

Some of the respondents commented upon the way in which careers was now being taken seriously in their schools and improvements taking place.

'Improving. No longer on the critical list. Needs a financial blood transfusion...'

Despite a reasonable selection of more positive remarks such as those above, the overwhelming majority of the comments received were highly critical of the state of careers which prevails in schools in 1986. All the comments received can be substantiated by the quantitative analysis which is given in this Report.

Some were totally dismissive about how their school values careers work:

'Careers in this school is a joke.'

Whilst others were more positive about the general state of things:

'I consider that careers work must be one of the most rewarding areas of teaching.'

Others looking, perhaps, to the future with the involvement of a more comprehensive range of staff from each school commented about the need to get rid of the 'one man band' approach.

'I look forward to the demise of the all-singing, all-dancing careers teacher.'

Perhaps the saddest comment of all comes from the careers teacher who is no longer prepared to accept the totally intolerable burden of demands and responsibilities placed upon them and wrote:

'Having sat down and analysed what I do, what time I am allowed, I realised what a fool I am. I am, therefore, with great regret leaving the profession of my choice after 20 years.'

All of the comments which were critical of the way in which careers is valued or viewed within the schools fell in one or more of 10 categories.

The largest single category of concern surrounds the whole question of **TIME**. How can careers teachers provide even an adequate service without a reasonable amount of time? It does not appear, from the responses, that the teachers are being unreasonable or that they want to be free of all other time constraints, but it is difficult to envisage how matters will improve unless due recognition is given, by all concerned, to the need to provide teachers with the time to do the job.

'In both time and resources, careers work has been pruned for the sake of the needs of others. Careers time has been cut out to introduce other subjects and because the careers teacher also teaches science, his time allocation to careers teaching has been very vulnerable.'

'Over the past few years the amount of time given to careers work has fallen.'

Whereas **TIME** was seen, at least numerically, as the single largest inhibitor of the development of careers work the lack of **TRAINING** was a very close second. It cannot be anything short of a national disgrace that a survey, such as this one, finds that 41% of careers teachers have received less than five days of in-service training. Imagine the outcry if a similar level of training was afforded to the country's secondary school teachers of English, science, mathematics, etc.

'I was trained to teach English and regard myself as an enthusiastic amateur and deplore my lack of specific job training.'

'I find the work fascinating and only wish I'd got better qualifications.'

There is a very definite feeling amongst careers teachers that their work within schools is very much under resourced, not just in terms of time which has already been highlighted, but particularly in terms of **EQUIPMENT AND RESOURCES**.

'Overworked and under-recognised re: time and resources given by the hierarchy.'

'Only this year provided with an external telephone line. Rental and charges borne by TVEI (shared with head of TVEI).'

Interlinked with **RESOURCES,** and in some cases impossible to differentiate, is the whole question of **FINANCE** for the careers department. In very many cases the allocation of capitation to the careers department is at best minimal.

'Too little money. Too little time. Responsibility without power.'

'Like everyone else I could be more effective with more financial support.'

'The financial allocation, while not decreasing, has not increased so it will not allow me to purchase as much.'

Most career teachers feel that their work in schools is very much under-valued. Many have little or no say in the development of the curriculum or in the management of the schools. Whilst a significant number are paid on a fairly senior salary scale few are accorded either the **STATUS** of that salary or in terms of the importance of the work which they undertake. This lack of status is generally seen as 'lip-service' to the nationally recognised importance of this area of secondary school work.

'Unless careers education is given the same status as other subjects in school both in time and finance we are just toying with the problems.'

Of course much of the criticism made stems directly from the attitude of the head of the school and/or the attitude of other members of staff. It is one thing for teachers to acknowledge the importance of careers work, but it is another for them, in a finite resource situation, to be prepared to see a more equitable allocation of the schools resources. This, of course, includes time for careers. There is, in addition, the problem of the lack of understanding which teachers, in general, have for the work of the careers department.

> 'Even the most 'experienced' of teachers think that the careers teachers just 'find jobs' for pupils!'

> 'Any attempt to include careers education or extend its influence upon the curriculum is basically blocked by the Headmaster.'

Another 'complaint' which careers teachers log is the one concerning the **OTHER DUTIES** for which they are responsible, in addition to the duties associated with running or helping to run a careers department. Indeed it is very significant that 64% of those teachers who are paid an allowance for doing careers work are expected, for the same money, to carry other positions of responsibility.

> 'Can't do it all at once especially when running the PE department as well.'

Very much linked to this issue is the problem of the already **FULL TIMETABLE**. This means much of the work has to be done in the teacher's own time.

> 'The careers teacher is head of humanities so has a shortage of time for the work (careers). So largely

an activity confined to early morning, lunch-time and after school. Difficulty in arranging contact with specific pupils requiring advice eg fifth year leavers.'

> 'Last year my colleague and I had to accept a 23% cut in our time for careers work. This was as a result of a 23% increase in our teaching load of other subjects.'

An area of concern raised by a minority of the respondents centred on the lack of any curriculum time for careers education. As the quantitative analysis shows there are still schools which offer no careers education to some fourth, some fifth and some sixth year pupils.

A number of comments were received about the involvement of the careers service in schools' careers work. Most of these comments were about the inadequate staffing levels - which meant schools were often without a careers officer - or the amount of time which the Principal Careers Officer allocated to schools work. Apart from contact with the careers officer(s) allocated to their school, careers teachers do not have very much, if any, contact with other members of the service.

Generally there is a great deal of optimism about the work, but the biggest single danger appears to be that careers teachers are likely to be swamped given the enormity of the task expected of them and the inadequacies of the system in providing them with the tools (time, training, finance, resources, status, etc) to carry out the task.

'The demands made upon careers teachers have increased even more and although I have a supportive Head, I sometimes find that my careers work threatens to take over my life!'

This page has been intentionally left blank

VI CONCLUSIONS

It was stated in the introduction to this Report that the Survey commissioned by NACGT was not an update of Survey 18 and that point needs to be reiterated. However, in trying to draw conclusions from this Survey it is difficult, if not impossible, not to make comparisons with the findings of Survey 18.

It could be argued, of course, that direct comparison should be made given that Survey 18 provides the only valid data bank against which we can measure progress in the careers field. Clearly to make comparisons based on finance becomes a fruitless exercise unless the costs of 1973 are altered to take into account inflation. (One only has to recall the cost of buying Survey 18 (68p) to realise what has happened to prices over the past 13 to 15 years.)

Some limited comparison is possible and, so I believe, quite legitimate. One main difference between the two Surveys which must be stated concerns the method used to present the data as well as the slight variation in the numbers of schools involved. For Survey 18 the DES 'targetted' a cross-section of schools so as to provide a representative sample. The exercise resulted in 1175 questionnaires being sent out which provided approximately a 20% sample. Some of the schools failed to return the questionnaire whilst others returned questionnaires which were unusable. The end result was that 94% of the sample

was used. Unlike the 1986 Survey, HMI followed up the questionnaire with visits to over 100 of the sample schools. The results from the questionnaire were weighted and the report gave an estimate for the whole country.

For the 1986 Survey a questionnaire was sent to (but not necessarily received by) all secondary schools, and over 900 completed questionnaires were returned, making approximately a 20% sample. The main difference between the two surveys, however, lies in the fact that the 1986 sample was completely random and the figures provided in this Report apply only to the schools used.

Nevertheless such is the similarity both of the answers to the questions and the size of the sample, that it is fairly safe to say that the results paint an accurate picture of the state of careers in the UK (excluding Ulster) in 1986.

Although it is claimed that 71% of the schools in the sample have a written policy statement for careers education it appears that the careers teachers in 3% of the schools do not know if such a written policy statement exists. This must raise questions about the status of careers in these schools.

Clearly confusion reigns when the question of an LEA written policy for careers education is discussed as 36% of schools do not know the answer to that question. Worse still is the fact that many careers teachers within the same authority gave conflicting answers to the same question. To a slightly lesser extent, the same response was received to the question about whether the LEA had an adviser/inspector with specific responsibility for careers education.

It can only be concluded that there exists a major breakdown in communication between LEAs and careers teachers.

From the data received it can be seen that increasing numbers of teachers are participating in school careers work. Whilst 70% of all those involved are designated as careers teachers, only 53% receive an allowance for undertaking the work. However, it can be further concluded that not all schools pay their senior careers teacher anything like the rate the job deserves. **For example 13% of schools (with the exception of those in Scotland) pay their senior careers teacher on Scale 1 or 2.** This is an appalling state of affairs.

Despite the fact that 83% of schools regard their senior careers teacher as a head of department, only just over half (52%) are usually or always involved in 'school management decisions'. Similarly, only 63% of the 'heads of careers' sit on the school's curriculum committee.

Schools adopting this policy may, of course, be influenced by the totally inadequate amount of training which most careers teachers have received. One wonders what would happen if teachers were appointed head of maths or head of English with less than five days of training in that subject.

Survey 18 commented on the 'pressing need' for an expanded in-service training programme. **The situation in 1986 is nothing short of a national disgrace. Immediate steps need to be taken to overcome the appalling situation which exists.**

From the statistical data obtained from the Survey it can be concluded that the finance allocated to careers departments is either very good or very bad. For example 5% of the careers departments receive less than £50 pa; 28% receive less than £150. However, 21% receive more than £400.

There do not appear to be any serious omissions as far as careers department resources are concerned. However, it is difficult to understand how a careers department can be effective without an outside telephone line; but certainly 32% of schools expect their careers departments to do just that.

The introduction of new technology, such as 'micros', into careers departments appears to be fairly slow with only 12% having their own micro and 16% not even having access to one.

Increasingly society, particularly employers, expects young people to enter the labour market well-equipped for a working life in an era of rapid technological change. **Yet the very department in a school which is central to the young person's transition from full-time compulsory education to the next** stage of their life is starved of the very equipment which we expect those young people to be able to use.

Linked to this point, there is only a very small number of schools who subscribe to either Prestel or TTNS. Presumably the high cost of the telephone charges is a very serious factor in inhibiting their use in schools. However, both these services ought to be used by careers departments.

Another area which gives rise to serious concern is that of careers information. Whilst 80% of respondents claim to instruct all students in the systematic use of careers information, only 42% have a careers information area totally accessible to the students. **Information which is inaccessible to the students can be of no use to them.**

Survey 18 described a very impoverished situation as far as the devotion of curriculum time to careers education was concerned. The situation in 1986 has changed drastically, but is still far from perfect, with third year students in 20% of schools receiving no careers education. This problem is compounded by the fact that in a further 11% of schools only selected third year students receive careers education. The situation in years four and five is only marginally better.

Despite all the publicity over the past decade, supporting the need for careers education, **large numbers of young people still do not receive this 'essential and integral part of the secondary school curriculum'.**

From the data received it can easily be concluded that 'heads of careers' have insufficient time to carry out the full range of tasks expected of them.

The medical analogy of the careers teacher being the general practitioner very much prevails. Careers teachers carry out a wide range of functions, but the majority spend less than 10% of their time on any of them. Even 'teaching careers' fits into this general principle.

The most worrying feature to be revealed on the subject of how heads of careers spend their time is that **56% spend more than 30% of it on non-careers activities.** Little wonder they find time scarce!

So acute is the shortage of time for the vast majority of heads of careers that they spend, on average, nearly seven hours a week of their own time on careers. **In other words they work a six-day week.**

It is probably safe to conclude that a significant factor in the 'time issue' is that clerical help is minimal and the heads of careers often end up having to carry out clerical tasks. This will be particularly true in such activities as organising work experience or careers conventions.

There do appear to be some anomalies in the use of student record systems. The fact that 19% of schools do not allow the careers service access to the careers department's student record system and 56% of schools do not allow the careers service access to the school's student record system is quite disturbing. Both are, after all, part of the education service. Even more intriguing is the fact that 7% of schools do not allow their head of careers access to the school's record system.

Given the paucity of in-service provision it is surprising that 'training courses' do not play a more significant part in the activities of local careers associations.

The main thrust of a careers officer's activity in schools lies in 'interviewing individual students', with 64% of careers officers spending over 70% of their time on this particular activity. All other careers officer activities take up a very small percentage of time - the norm being up to 5% of their time. However, this must be seen in context particularly given the relatively small amount of careers officer time which schools allegedly receive.

Apart from the careers officer allocated to a particular school it is possible to conclude that the school is very unlikely to receive a visit from any other member of the careers service.

Between 50% and 82% of schools claim never to receive a visit from other members of the careers service. The percentage varies with the role of the particular members of staff. It is significant that 13% of schools do not organise work experience for students, and only 64% of those that do promote a policy of it being 'open and available to all students'. Employer contact with schools, not including work experience, appears to be good. With only 9% of schools having regular meetings between staff and the staff of colleges of further education, there is room for a great deal of improvement in this sphere.

It can be concluded that schools are making significant efforts to encourage both parents and former pupils to participate in the 'careers process'. This is good although, clearly, there continues to be room for improvement.

Thanks to the efforts of over 900 careers teachers we are able to make some conclusions about 'the state of careers in 1986'. There has been considerable improvement over the years, particularly since the publication of Survey 18 in 1973. However, there is still a long way to go, particularly as far as training, curriculum time for careers education and time for the heads of careers are concerned.

Hopefully there will be a continued upsurge in support of the work of careers teachers and the shortcomings of 1986 will be overcome by the end of the decade.

VII RECOMMENDATIONS

Repeatedly, for more than a decade, central government, amongst others, has extolled the virtues of ensuring that quality careers education and guidance is available to young people in the latter years of secondary education. Clearly, as the data obtained from over 900 schools reveals, the current situation is far from ideal. The analysis of this Survey, undertaken by David Cleaton, highlights serious gaps in the careers provision for our young people, and the NACGT believes that both central and local government must take instant steps to remedy the more impoverished areas of careers work.

The Association, therefore, wishes to make the following recommendations which it believes will do much towards raising the level of provision to the point at which, it would appear, central government and certainly members of this Association believe it should be.

1   We recommend that central government through the Department of Education and Science:

   (a) implement the recommendations of the Report of Her Majesty's Inspectors of Schools, Survey 18, particularly that section relating to the in-service training of careers teachers;

   (b) introduce an emergency training programme, centrally funded, so that careers teachers are afforded the level of training necessary to carry out the functions of the job;

   (c) implement the proposal made in the White Paper, jointly published by the DES and Department of Employment, 'Working Together - Education and Training' (July 1986) which proposed that all LEAs should produce 'Guidelines for Careers Education';

   (d) advise LEAs of the importance of having an adviser/inspector with specific responsibility for careers education and that such a person should have the necessary training and experience to undertake the duties of the post;

   (e) publicise the importance of all students receiving, as part of their curriculum from the third year upwards, a regular input of careers education. (This Association accepts that it may not be called careers education, but should include the main ingredients of a comprehensive programme of social and personal education);

   (f) recommend to LEAs and schools that a minimum of one hour per week of the curriculum be designated for careers education (or whatever it may be termed);

   (g) acknowledge the enormous amount of their own time which careers teachers devote to careers work and recommend their inclusion in the designation of any senior posts which may become part of a new salary structure for teachers.

2   We further recommend that central government, through the careers service branch of the Department of Employment, in publishing guidelines for the work of the careers service:

(a) ensure that sufficient importance is given to the need for LEAs to provide a reasonable amount of careers officer time to be spent at school;

(b) ensure that interviewing is not the sole purpose of careers officers visiting schools;

(c) ensure that members of careers service staff, other than the careers officer for the school, regularly visit schools within the authority.

3   We recommend that local education authorities should:

(a) publish, annually, a 'policy statement for careers education';

(b) ensure that all schools receive a copy of their guidelines and that the philosophy contained therein is disseminated to all teachers and careers officers;

(c) employ an adviser/inspector with specific responsibility for careers education, with the necessary experience and training to undertake the task;

(d) acknowledge that careers teachers are professional educators and should not be employed in clerical tasks for which clerical support should be provided.

4   We recommend that schools:

(a) give due regard to the importance of careers education;

(b) provide time for both teachers and pupils so that the process of careers education and guidance is allowed to flourish;

(c) remember the value of using, to the fullest extent, their local employers, parents, local colleges and former students;

(d) establish a closer working relationship with colleges of further education and, at least, ensure that regular meetings are held between the most relevant staff.

5   Finally we recommend that all those involved in providing and supporting careers education and guidance for our young people should work closely together. We are of the firm opinion that an example can be set by the more obvious collaboration of government departments such as the DES, the Department of Employment, MSC, etc and that the time is ripe for the establishment of a more comprehensive government department – the Department of Education and Training, which would oversee the education and training of 14-19 year olds.

VIII APPENDICES

1 BIBLIOGRAPHY

Careers Education in Secondary Schools – Education Survey 18,
Department of Education and Science (HMSO) 1973

1.1 What is the size of the school?

Less than 750 students ☐   750 – 1200 ☐   1201 – 1500 ☐

1501 – 2000 ☐   2000 + ☐

1.2 What is the age range of the students?

11 (or 12) – 18 yrs ☐   11 (or 12) – 16 ☐   11 – 14 ☐

13 – 18 ☐   14 – 18 ☐   16 + ☐

1.3 What is the designation of the school?

Comprehensive ☐   Secondary Modern ☐   Grammar ☐   Special ☐

Independent ☐   6th Form College ☐   Single sex female ☐   Single sex male ☐

Co-educational ☐   Tertiary College ☐

1.4 How would you describe the school's catchment area?

Rural ☐   Mostly rural ☐   Mostly urban ☐   Urban ☐

Seaside ☐

1.5 Does the school participate in TVEI?   YES ☐ NO ☐

1.6 Does the school provide CPVE courses?   YES ☐ NO ☐

1.7 Does the school have a written policy statement for careers education?   YES ☐ NO ☐ DON'T KNOW ☐

1.8 Which l.e.a.?

1.9 Does the l.e.a. have a written policy statement for careers education?   YES ☐ NO ☐ DON'T KNOW ☐

1.10 Is there an l.e.a. adviser/inspector with specific responsibility for careers education?   YES ☐ NO ☐ DON'T KNOW ☐

If YES is this a shared responsibility for another subject?   YES ☐ NO ☐

2.1 **How many of the school's teaching staff are formally involved in careers work?**

1 ☐ 2 ☐ 3 ☐ 4 ☐ 5 ☐ 6 ☐ 7 ☐ 8 ☐ 9 ☐ 10 ☐

More ☐

2.2 **How many of these are designated careers teachers?** ☐

2.3 **How many are members of NACGT?** 1/ 2/ 3/ 4/ 5

2.4 **How many are paid an allowance specifically for undertaking careers work?** ☐

2.5 **What scale is the senior careers teacher paid?** ☐ Is this purely for careers work? YES ☐ NO ☐

2.6 **Is the senior careers teacher regarded as a Head of Department?** YES ☐ NO ☐

2.7 **DOES THE HEAD OF CAREERS**

	always	usually	rarely	never
Participate in school management decisions	☐	☐	☐	☐
Sit on the school's curriculum committee (or equivalent)	☐	☐	☐	☐

2.8 **What is the number of full-time equivalent careers teachers in the school?**

Less than 1 ☐ 1 or more, but not more than 2 ☐ 2 or more, but not more than 3 ☐

3 or more, but not more than 4 ☐ 4 or more ☐

2.9 **How much training have the staff in 2.2 received?** (Please use a 'C' for any staff currently involved in course of training)

	No. of staff					
	1	2	3	4	5	>5
Less than 5 days	☐	☐	☐	☐	☐	☐
Between 5 and 20 days	☐	☐	☐	☐	☐	☐
Between 21 and 50 days	☐	☐	☐	☐	☐	☐
A f/t course of 1 term	☐	☐	☐	☐	☐	☐
A f/t course of 1 year	☐	☐	☐	☐	☐	☐
A p/t course of less than 1 year	☐	☐	☐	☐	☐	☐
A p/t course of at least 1 year	☐	☐	☐	☐	☐	☐

3.1 **How much finance was allocated to the careers department for 1985-86 academic year?**

Up to £50 ☐   Between £51 and £100 ☐   Between £101 and £150 ☐
Between £151 and £200 ☐   Between £201 and £250 ☐   Between £251 and £300 ☐
Between £301 and £351 ☐   Between £351 and £400 ☐   More than £400 ☐

Is the capitation supplemented by help from other departments   YES ☐   NO ☐
or central pool   YES ☐   NO ☐

3.2 **Does the careers department have the following?**

	YES	NO		YES	NO
A careers classroom	☐	☐	A separate careers library	☐	☐
A separate office for HOD	☐	☐	A display area for vacancies & YTS opportunities	☐	☐
An interview room	☐	☐	An external telephone line	☐	☐
Storage space	☐	☐	An internal telephone line	☐	☐
A careers display area	☐	☐			

3.3 **What equipment is available and to what extent is it used?**

	Exclusively by careers dept.	Available	Not available	Used regularly	Used	Never used
Radio	☐	☐	☐	☐	☐	☐
T.V.	☐	☐	☐	☐	☐	☐
Video machine	☐	☐	☐	☐	☐	☐
Overhead projector	☐	☐	☐	☐	☐	☐
Microprocessor/computer	☐	☐	☐	☐	☐	☐
Film projector	☐	☐	☐	☐	☐	☐

3.4 **Does the school subscribe to Prestel**   YES ☐ NO ☐   Times Network System   YES ☐ NO ☐

3.5 **Is the careers information area**

Totally accessible to students ☐   Available at certain times ☐   Only available on request ☐

3.6 **Are all students instructed in the systematic use of careers information**   YES ☐ NO ☐

4.1 **What is the organisation of classroom careers work?**

	For all students	Careers Education for some students	For no students
YEAR 1	☐	☐	☐
YEAR 2	☐	☐	☐
YEAR 3	☐	☐	☐
YEAR 4	☐	☐	☐
YEAR 5	☐	☐	☐
6TH FORM	☐	☐	☐

4.2 **Where curriculum time is allocated to careers what is the average number of hours (per year) of careers education each student receives in:**

	UP TO 10 HRS	11 – 20 HRS	21 – 30 HRS	31 – 40 HRS	MORE THAN 40 HRS
YEAR 1	☐	☐	☐	☐	☐
YEAR 2	☐	☐	☐	☐	☐
YEAR 3	☐	☐	☐	☐	☐
YEAR 4	☐	☐	☐	☐	☐
YEAR 5	☐	☐	☐	☐	☐
6th FORM	☐	☐	☐	☐	☐

4.3 **Does careers education stand as a subject on its own** ☐

or as part of Social and Personal Education (or equivalent) ☐

or as part of another subject ☐

4.4 **Does the school use the JIG/CAL system?**　　YES ☐　　　　NO ☐

5.1 **(a) How much non-teaching time is allocated to the Head of Careers?**

Up to 3 hrs p.w. ☐	4 – 6 hrs p.w. ☐	6 – 9 hrs p.w. ☐
9 – 12 hrs p.w. ☐	12 – 15 hrs p.w. ☐	More than 15 hrs p.w. ☐

(b) How much of this time is specifically for careers?

Up to 3 hrs p.w. ☐	4 – 6 hrs p.w. ☐	6 – 9 hrs p.w. ☐
9 – 12 hrs p.w. ☐	12 – 15 hrs p.w. ☐	More than 15 hrs p.w. ☐
not specified ☐		

(c) What is the total amount of non-teaching time allocated to staff specifically for careers work?

Up to 5 hrs p.w. ☐	6 – 10 hrs p.w. ☐	11 – 15 hrs p.w. ☐
16 – 20 hrs p.w. ☐	21 – 25 hrs p.w. ☐	More than 25 hrs p.w. ☐

5.2 **On the basis of an annual average how is the time of the Head of Careers divided up?**

	0%	Up to 5%	6 – 10%	11 – 15%	16 – 20%	21% – 25%	26% – 30%	Over 30%
Teaching "careers"	☐	☐	☐	☐	☐	☐	☐	☐
Interviewing	☐	☐	☐	☐	☐	☐	☐	☐
Organising information	☐	☐	☐	☐	☐	☐	☐	☐
Helping colleages	☐	☐	☐	☐	☐	☐	☐	☐
Liaison with the Careers Service	☐	☐	☐	☐	☐	☐	☐	☐
Visiting	☐	☐	☐	☐	☐	☐	☐	☐
General administration	☐	☐	☐	☐	☐	☐	☐	☐
Preparing careers material	☐	☐	☐	☐	☐	☐	☐	☐
Keeping up-to-date	☐	☐	☐	☐	☐	☐	☐	☐
Other careers activities	☐	☐	☐	☐	☐	☐	☐	☐
Non-careers activities	☐	☐	☐	☐	☐	☐	☐	☐

5.3 **On average, how many hours of his/her own time does the Head of Careers give to the dept. each week?** ☐

5.4 Is clerical/secretarial help available to the careers department?   YES ☐   NO ☐

If YES – is a specific amount of time allocated to the Careers Department   YES ☐   NO ☐

If YES – how much   Up to 5 hrs p.w. ☐   6 – 10 hrs p.w. ☐   11 – 15 hrs p.w. ☐
    16 – 20 hrs p.w. ☐   21 – 25 hrs p.w. ☐   More than 25 hrs p .w. ☐

5.5 (a) Does the Careers Department maintain a student record system of its own?   YES ☐   NO ☐
(b) IF YES – does the Careers Service have open access to this system?   YES ☐   NO ☐
(c) Does the school have a student record system?   YES ☐   NO ☐
(d) If YES – does the Careers Department have direct access to the school's pupil record system?   YES ☐   NO ☐
(e) Does the Careers Service have the same access?   YES ☐   NO ☐

5.6 Does the school have a "pupil profile" system?   YES ☐   NO ☐

Does the Careers Department participate in this?
    In a minor way ☐   Same as any other department ☐   In a major way ☐

5.7 Does the school operate a 3rd Year "Options" system?   YES ☐   NO ☐

If YES – what is the Careers Department's involvement in the system   A major contributor ☐   Same as any other department ☐
    A minor role ☐   No part ☐

5.8 Does the careers department produce a booklet/information on the occupational significance of choosing particular subjects.
    ☐ YES   ☐ NO

6.1 LOCAL CAREERS ASSOCIATION

Is there a local careers association   YES ☐   NO ☐

If YES   Is your attendance at meetings – Regular ☐   Frequent ☐   Rare ☐   Not at all ☐

In what activities does the association participate –

Training courses ☐   Topical discussions ☐   Visits to industry/commerce/f.e. ☐

Co-ordination of work experience schemes ☐   Sharing resources ☐   Don't know ☐

Writing of curriculum materials ☐   Evaluating materials ☐

Liaison with the Careers Service ☐   To write and agree policy statements ☐

6.2 CAREERS SERVICE

(a) How many careers officers work with the school on a regular basis

None ☐   One ☐   Two ☐   Three ☐   Four ☐   Five ☐

(b) What is the average weekly total amount of careers officer time allocated to the school

Up to 5 hrs p.w. ☐   6 – 10 hrs p.w. ☐   11 – 15 hrs p.w. ☐   16 – 20 hrs p.w. ☐

21 – 25 hrs p.w. ☐   More than 25 hrs p.w. ☐

(c) How is the careers officer time given to the school divided-up?

	0%	Up to 5%	6 – 10%	11 – 20%	21 – 30%	31 – 40%	41 – 50%	51 – 60%	61 – 70%	More than 70%
Interviewing individual students	☐	☐	☐	☐	☐	☐	☐	☐	☐	☐
Interviewing group of students	☐	☐	☐	☐	☐	☐	☐	☐	☐	☐
"Teaching" careers	☐	☐	☐	☐	☐	☐	☐	☐	☐	☐
Talking to parents	☐	☐	☐	☐	☐	☐	☐	☐	☐	☐
Advising staff	☐	☐	☐	☐	☐	☐	☐	☐	☐	☐
Organising work experience	☐	☐	☐	☐	☐	☐	☐	☐	☐	☐
Visiting students on work exp.	☐	☐	☐	☐	☐	☐	☐	☐	☐	☐
Organising careers library	☐	☐	☐	☐	☐	☐	☐	☐	☐	☐
Training staff	☐	☐	☐	☐	☐	☐	☐	☐	☐	☐
Helping with 3rd Yr. Options	☐	☐	☐	☐	☐	☐	☐	☐	☐	☐
Other	☐	☐	☐	☐	☐	☐	☐	☐	☐	☐

6.2 cont

(d) Do other members of the Careers Service visit the school?

	Regularly	Occasionally	Rarely	Never
Employment Officer/Asst.	☐	☐	☐	☐
C.S. Information Officer	☐	☐	☐	☐
Older leaver/more able C.O.	☐	☐	☐	☐
Unemployment specialist	☐	☐	☐	☐
Special Needs C.O.	☐	☐	☐	☐
Other specialists	☐	☐	☐	☐
Head of the Service	☐	☐	☐	☐

(e) Where is the nearest careers office?

At your Institution	☐
In the same town	☐
Not in the same town but within 10 miles	☐
More than 10 miles away	☐

(f) Does the Careers Service

	Regularly	Occasionally	Rarely	Never
Provide local careers information	☐	☐	☐	☐
Provide details of employment/training courses for yp eg. YTS	☐	☐	☐	☐
Arrange training courses for teachers	☐	☐	☐	☐
Invite teachers to join in visits to employers	☐	☐	☐	☐
Organise or offer administrative support for a local careers assoc.	☐	☐	☐	☐

(g) Does the Careers Service provide a careers education material resource centre   YES ☐   NO ☐

If YES, can the materials be borrowed?   YES ☐   NO ☐

6.3 EMPLOYERS

(a) Does the school have regular contact with a wide range of employers and/or employer organisation and/or training organisations?   YES ☐   NO ☐

(b) Is this contact mainly with   the careers dept. ☐   Mainly other depts. ☐   Roughly equal ☐

(c) Do employers participate in the schools careers work?   Frequently ☐   Fairly regularly ☐   Rarely ☐   Never ☐

(d) Do students participate in work experience schemes (i) Organised by the school   YES ☐   NO ☐
                                                        (ii) Organised from outside the school   YES ☐   NO ☐

(e) If YES, how would you describe the policy for work experience   Open and available to all students ☐
                                                                      Open only to particular groups of students ☐

(f) (i) How many students took part in work experience during the last academic year? ☐
    (ii) How many employers took part in the same period? ☐

(g) Approximately how many employers does the careers department have contact with during a year? (not including work experience)

	None ☐	Up to 10 ☐	11 – 20 ☐
	21 – 30 ☐	31 – 40 ☐	41 – 50 ☐
	More than 50 ☐		

(h) Does the school hold a careers convention?   Never ☐ Occasionally ☐ Every 2 years ☐ Every year ☐

(i) Approximately how many employers participate in the convention ☐

6.4 FURTHER EDUCATION

(a) What % of students transferred from your school at 16 to f.e. college at the end of the 1984/5 academic year? ☐

(b) How are the students informed about f.e. courses?

By the school ☐   College prospectus ☐   Careers convention ☐
College lecturers visiting the school ☐   Students visiting the colleges ☐   By the careers office ☐
Other ☐

(c) Are meetings between school staff and college staff held
Regularly ☐ Occasionally ☐ Rarely ☐ Never ☐

6.5 HIGHER EDUCATION

(a) What % of students from your school went directly on to higher education at the beginning of the 1985 academic year [   ]

(b) How are the students informed about higher education courses

By the school [   ] University/polytechnic prospectus [   ] Careers Conventions [   ] H.E. Convention [   ]

H.E. lecturers visiting the school [   ] Students visiting H.E. institutions [   ] By Careers Service [   ] Other [   ]

6.6 PARENTS

(a) What are the main methods used by the careers department to communicate with parents

Regular newsletter [   ] Parents evenings about careers [   ] Open days [   ] Individual personal letters [   ]

By word of mouth through students [   ] Other [   ]

(b) Are parents formally used in the careers process

Extensively [   ] Occasionally [   ] Rarely [   ] Never [   ]

6.7 FORMER STUDENTS

(a) Is any attempt made to use the experience of former students in the careers process YES [   ] NO [   ]

(b) If YES, how is this done?

By inviting specific individual former students back into school for the purpose [   ]

Leaving it to chance to see if anyone returns; using them where possible [   ]

Hoping employers will use former students in links with the school [   ]

Other [   ]

Please specify:

Please write any comments, observations etc. that you want to make about the state of careers work in your school.

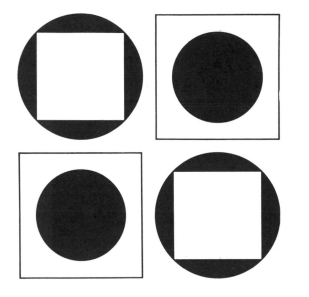

THE SIGN
THAT MEANS
GOOD PRACTICE
IN CAREERS
EDUCATION
AND GUIDANCE

NACGT   The National Association of Careers & Guidance Teachers

WHAT DO WE DO?

The NACGT:

- promotes the development of careers education and guidance for all young people in secondary and tertiary education
- has meetings with the Secretary of State for Education and Science, the Minister of State for Employment, Opposition Parties and HMI – to ensure that the views of members are heard
- organises a national conference annually on current topics with nationally known speakers
- keeps its members informed of recent developments in the field through publications
- has a regional structure to encourage local contacts and communication
- has representation, through elected representatives, on many national bodies eg COIC, BTEC, EITB, NICEC, CECS
- offers its own training courses (organised by senior members of Council).

WHAT DO WE OFFER?

As a member you would receive:

- the 'Annual Guide'

- 'The Careers and Guidance Teacher' - a termly journal

- frequent newsletters

- information sheets

- 'Skill-Share' - an 'ideas' paper

- free advice

- reduced rates for NACGT training courses and the annual
  conference

- information on events organised by regional committees

- 'Updates' - short papers from practitioners.

Don't feel you have to work in isolation - join us and share your problems with others who have faced them before. Pick up new ideas. Keep informed, exchange news and views and add to your expertise.

HOW TO JOIN?

You can join for an annual subscription of £15 (this can be set against income tax - or paid by your employer).

WANT TO KNOW MORE?

Then write to: Mrs Gwen L Stanton
                      Membership Secretary NACGT
                      46 Fairfield Road
                      Penarth
                      South Glamorgan CF6 1SL

4 THE NEWPOINT PUBLISHING COMPANY LIMITED

Early in 1986 the Newpoint Publishing Group of Companies, incorporating The New Opportunity Press (by which name we were previously better known to you), rationalised over 15 years of experience as market leaders in the provision of up-to-date information and high quality products concerned with career/ life planning and development into one company - The Newpoint Publishing Company Limited.

Our catalogue bears witness to that experience, in the continued publication of well-respected titles such as Graduate Opportunities (GO) and Which Degree, the development and expansion of the Job Knowledge Index (JKI) and our new publications at school and college leaver level, Focus at 16 and Focus at 18 (born out of work on the long-established and respected Opportunities for School Leavers) - together with new ventures in specific areas of interest, as well as in topics affecting the learning process of readers at any age.

The 1987 Catalogue of Publications, Materials and Services contains full details of our whole range of products and future projects, integral to any involvement or interest in the world of work and education, dealing as they do with work and life skills which have much more far-reaching implications and importance than simply for career building.

TO OBTAIN YOUR COPY OF THE NEWPOINT CATALOGUE

Either write to: The Newpoint Publishing Company Ltd
                      Department CS
                      Newpoint House
                      St James' Lane
                      London N10 3DF

or ring Book
Marketing on: 01 444 7281.